D0101765

SECONDHAND AND VINTAGE

LONDON

Andrew Whittaker

Vivays Publishing

Thank you and love to Emma, always
encouraging. And a big thanks to
London's secondhand and vintage
traders, whose help and enthusiasm
made compiling this book such an
enjoyable experience.

Published by Vivays Publishing Ltd

www.vivays-publishing.com

A catalogue record for this book is
available from the British Library

ISBN 978-1-908126-19-1

Publishing Director: Lee Ripley
Design: Draught Associates
Cover image: Parul Arora
Map data: ©OpenStreetMap (and) contributors, CC-BY-SA

Printed in China

LONDON
CONTENTS

LONDON
HOW TO USE THIS BOOK

Each chapter in *Secondhand and Vintage London* has a theme. The first three are categorised by goods – Clothes & Accessories; Books, Music & Memorabilia; and Home & Garden. Chapter four, Only in London, covers the markets, auctions and car boot sales.

The entries within each chapter are arranged by location. Each includes a description of the shop or market, alongside contact details, opening times and a guide to the relative price of the goods, set on a scale from £ to £££ (from bargain to investment).

A section of maps in the second half of the book show you where to find the shops and markets, with each trader marked by a coloured diamond. The colour of the diamonds on the maps corresponds to the chapter colourings. These maps also provide a link to the internet that can be accessed through your smartphone.

INTRODUCTION

London has thousands of secondhand and vintage shops. They draw you in – thrift, recycling and the simple, magical allure of old things all playing a part. It's not like normal shopping. There is no uniformity, no certainty. Instead, shopping for secondhand and vintage in London is an adventure, a journey of discovery that takes you to some of the city's most individual shops, found in its most atmospheric quarters.

The city has always had a good line in secondhand merchandise, going all the way back to the medieval traders who dealt in cast-off clothes on London Bridge. Of course it's evolved tremendously in the intervening centuries, no more so than in the last 20 years. Today, secondhand shopping in London is a multilayered affair, embracing sustainability and style alongside the old traditions of frugality.

It remains closest to its medieval roots in the city's innumerable charity shops, or at the markets and boot sales that unfurl in car parks and on patches of waste ground at weekends. Then there are the hundreds of specialist shops selling used books, clothes, furniture and anything else you can think of. Within these creative, endlessly varied shops, London has embraced the 21st century rise of 'vintage', a term given to goods that date from anywhere between 1910 and 1990 but which, in common, are retained for their design and quality. Remember – all vintage is secondhand, but not all secondhand is vintage. Vintage is a mid-century modern desk, or a silk chiffon flapper dress. Secondhand is a 1980s Yamaha keyboard or maybe a dog-eared Penguin reprint of *Wuthering Heights*. All of which, incidentally, are on sale somewhere in London right now.

The multiple layers of secondhand London continue to shift, a process keenly felt in the city's marketplaces. A handful of traditional secondhand markets remain, evoking the thrifty London of old. They sell used power tools, furniture, washing machines, shoes and anything else with a past life. They're cheap, completely engaging and, sadly, endangered – many have shut down in recent years.

By contrast, at London's growing roll call of vintage fairs and markets, the clothes, furniture and other goods are more carefully edited (the sifting has been done for you), and the prices correspondingly higher. Some markets meet in the middle, mixing good old fashioned secondhand with savvy vintage. In common, all of London's secondhand markets are colourful, friendly and exciting places to be.

Beyond the secondhand and vintage shops and markets lie the antique dealers, and London isn't short of fine antique shops. However, you won't find them in this book. Nor will you find the multitude of charity shops. Instead, *Secondhand and Vintage London* concentrates on the shops and markets that fall between the two extremes. We've tried to give a varied selection of traders, from dealers in old advertising posters to secondhand bike specialists. All of them are within easy reach of central London by bus or Tube.

So, dive in, explore the secondhand shops, meet the traders and get to know London a little better. It's an enriching experience. Just don't blame us when you leave a market or shop clutching a gaudy ceramic fish that just 'called out' to you – it's all part of the adventure.

CLOTHES & ACCESSORIES

Men's and Women's Garments
Hats / Bags and Belts
Shoes / Jewellery / Watches
Eyeglasses

THERE USED TO BE A CERTAIN STIGMA ATTACHED TO BUYING SECONDHAND CLOTHES. A REPUTATION FOR RIPS, SMELLS AND STAINS (EVEN MOTHS) THAT WAS HARD TO SHAKE. BUT THE SCENE HAS CHANGED DRAMATICALLY IN THE LAST 15 YEARS. LONDON HAS EMBRACED VINTAGE WITH VIGOUR, FROM GINGHAM TO GUCCI, CELEBRATING THE STYLE AND TAILORING OF DECADES PAST AND FUSING IT WITH CONTEMPORARY FASHIONS TO CREATE SOMETHING NEW.

Some secondhand clothes shops now buy their stock in bulk, wholesale style. Where they do, you're as likely to hear the word 'retro' as 'vintage'. Most, however, still source from auctions, from individual suppliers in hotspots outside London and, of course, from members of the public who sell their cast-offs over the counter. Among these shops, some specialise in either men's or women's clothes; others in a particular period or a genre, such as 'classic British' with its tweeds and waxy jackets; a number sell only designer clothes; and a few combine clothes with objects for the home and furniture, selling vintage as a lifestyle.

The prices can vary significantly from shop to shop (often dependent on which part of London you're in), although rare, designer or bespoke secondhand clothes are almost always identified and priced accordingly (and are still much cheaper than buying new!).

Keep an eye out for rips and marks (these clothes do have a past life) and always try on before you buy – sizings have changed over the years. Some of London's vintage shops offer an adjustment service so there is room for manoeuvre if the garments aren't a perfect fit.

Most of the shops explored in this chapter sell shoes and bags, and many also have accessories – from sunglasses to gloves and costume jewellery – alongside the clothes, but we have also listed a handful of jewellery shops with particularly interesting secondhand stock.

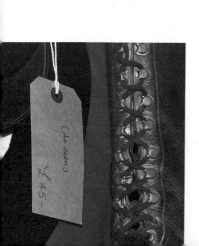

⊕⊕⊕
AUSTIN KAYE

425 Strand WC2R OQE
0207 240 1888
www.austinkaye.co.uk
Mon-Fri 9:30-17:30; Sat 9.30-17:00
Charing Cross Tube

The Kaye family shop has been selling watches on the Strand since 1946. Majoring on secondhand timepieces, it deals in everything from vintage Asprey pocket watches to Rolex wristwatches manufactured within the last five years. The range is staggering, and everything, naturally, is guaranteed.

⊕⊕£
BLACKOUT II

51 Endell Street, Covent Garden WC2H 9AJ
0207 240 5006
www.blackout2.com
Mon-Fri 11:00-19:00; Sat 11:30-18:30;
Sun 12:00-17:00
Tottenham Court Road/Covent Garden Tube

A shop which, like Radio Days in Waterloo and Camden's A Dandy in Aspic, buys into the idea of vintage as a lifestyle choice. Set over two floors, some of the clothes date back to the 1920s. Men and women are both catered for, although the latter have more to enjoy with a good selection of costume jewellery, handbags and vintage lingerie.

DIANE HARBY

£££-£££

148 Grays Antiques Market, Davies Street,
Mayfair W1K 5LP
0207 629 5130
Mon-Fri 10:00-18:00
Bond Street Tube

The production of fine lace has dwindled
away over the years. Much of the really
good stuff was made by child workers
(smaller hands you see) or nuns, neither of
whom are as common as they once were.
Diane Harby's shop sells this delicate old
material in the shape of shawls, stoles,
tableware, hankies and collars made
between the 1870s and the 1930s. The
quality and rarity of the items ensures
that most have been lovingly cared for
over the years. Diane also sells a handful
of clothes made from recycled pieces
of lace.

●●£-●●●

DOLLY DIAMOND

51 Pembridge Road,
Notting Hill Gate W11 3HG
0207 792 2479
www.dollydiamond.com
Mon-Fri 10:30-18:30; Sat 9:30-18:30;
Sun 12:00-18:00
Notting Hill Gate Tube

The friendly team at Dolly Diamond, one
of a cluster of secondhand clothiers in
Notting Hill Gate, describe their clothes
as 'proper vintage'. By that they mean
they're hand picked and in fine condition,
and that they date from the Victorian era
to the 1970s. It's a place to look for that
genuine 1920s silk chiffon flapper dress.
And to part with £600 when you decide
you can't live without it. Eveningwear is
a speciality, but they also sell bridal wear,
children's clothes and menswear.

●●£-●●●

FUR COAT NO KNICKERS

Top Floor, Kingly Court,
Carnaby Street W1B 5PW
07814 002295
www.furcoatnoknickers.co.uk
Mon-Sat 11:00-19:00 (Tue 11:00-17:30);
Sun 12:30-17:00
Oxford Circus Tube

A bright, unusual shop on the top floor
of Kingly Court, Fur Coat No Knickers
sells wedding dresses. They include the
genuine, vintage article made for some
lucky bride as far back in time as the
1930s; and others that are simply vintage
dresses capable of carrying off the big day,
for bride or guest. The shop also makes
exquisite dresses to measure, based on a
number of vintage shapes. Accessories,
from elegant old evening bags and
costume jewellery to tiaras and shawls,
complete the vintage wedding look.

HORNETS

**36B Kensington Church Street W8 4BX,
and 2&4 Kensington Church Walk W8 4NB
0207 938 4949/0207 937 2627
www.hornetskensington.co.uk
Mon-Sat 11:00-18:00
High Street Kensington Tube**

Remember when men were men? When they wore suits, hats and liberal amounts of tweed? Bill Hornets does. "We're talking about style not fashion," he explains, outlining the ethos behind the three small Kensington shops that comprise Hornets. "Classic, English, masculine clothes. We love Savile Row, we love good tailoring, we love Lobb shoes." The shop up on Kensington Church Street concentrates on daywear, including morning suits and tweed jackets; the two on Church Walk, in converted Georgian stables, have more in the way of eveningwear, with shirts, cravats, dinner jackets and more, all of it well preserved.

GILLIAN HORSRUP

**Inside Vintage Modes, Grays Antique Market,
1-7 Davies Mews, Mayfair W1K 5AB
0207 499 8121
www.gillianhorsup.com
Mon-Sat 11:00-17:00
Bond Street Tube**

Gillian has been selling jewellery around London's markets for three decades. Today, she has residency in The Mews annex of Grays Antique Market where she stocks an eclectic mix of costume jewellery, bags, compacts and other accessories. Art deco is a particular speciality. *Vogue*, *Tatler* and *Marie Claire* have all used Gillian's stock in photo shoots. "I like pieces that say immediately what era they're from," she says. "Whether that's a pair of sunglasses from the 50s or a 1980s bangle."

JANE BOURVIS

89 Golborne Road, Notting Hill W10 5NL
0208 964 5603
www.janebourvis.co.uk
Tue-Sat 10:30-18:00
Westbourne Park/Ladbroke Grove Tube

The pieces of bridal and occasion wear at Jane Bourvis' are unique. Many date back to the Victorian and Edwardian era; others are newly cut from the most delicate antique laces and textiles. Corsets, silk and silk brocade skirts, velvet and silk jackets and coats and vintage jewellery are also sold here. Little wonder that the shop's collection of outfits has shown at the V&A.

MARSHMALLOW MOUNTAIN

Ground Floor, Kingly court (off Carnaby St), London W1B 5PW
0207 434 9498
www.marshmallowmountain.com
Mon-Wed 11:00-19:00;
Thu-Sat 11:00-20:00, Sun 12:00-18:00
Oxford Circus/Piccadilly Circus Tube

A small, elegant vintage women's clothes and accessories shop that promises a 'boudoir' experience, inspired, as it was, by the owner's private salon parties. Most of the diligently selected stock is classic, some of it from coveted labels. The boot collection is rightfully renowned.

ONE OF A KIND

259 Portobello Road, Notting Hill W11 1LR
0207 792 5853
www.1kind.com
Mon-Sun 10:00-18:00 (18:30 on Sat)
Ladbroke Grove Tube

At first glance One of a Kind, stuffed wall-to-wall with men's and women's clothes, looks like many of the other 'vintage' shops that have sprung up in London in the past decade. However, observe the gallery of celebrity patrons behind the counter, Kate Moss and Sienna Miller amongst them, or pick something from the racks, and it becomes clear that much of the stock is high-end fashion, with labels and prices set accordingly. A mirror at the back of the shop conceals a door, opened by appointment only, behind which the owner has a collection patronised by Oscar-goers and socialites. It's the place to go for that genuine 1960s Pierre Cardin dress. Another back room is lined with shoes by Helmut Lang, Armani and others. Despite the kudos and prices, the shop and staff are down-to-earth, friendly and happy to chat.

ORSINI

76 Earls Court Road, Kensington W8 6EQ
0207 937 2903
Mon-Sat 10:30-18:00; Sun 12:00-17:00
High Street Kensington Tube

The clothes in Orsini are worthy of the V&A. The earliest, such as a black lace flapper dress, are nearly a century old. Other items are more recent, but no less historic, like the dresses from Ossie Clark, Leonard and Pucci. Some of the designer garments are non-vintage, drawn from collections only six months old. Non-designer outfits, such as 1950s day dresses and party dresses from the 1960s, are also sold, alongside vintage fur, jewellery and skin bags.

RELLIK

8 Golborne Road, Notting Hill W10 5NW
0208 962 0089
www.relliklondon.co.uk
Tue-Sat 10:00-18:00
Westbourne Park/Ladbroke Grove Tube

Rellik has been selling secondhand women's designer clothes in the shadow of the Trellick Tower for a decade, having moved from a market stall on nearby Portobello Road. The stock is refined, majoring in particular on British designers like Vivienne Westwood and Ossie Clark. Ring the bell to gain entry (unless you're Kylie or Kate, in which case they probably know you're coming).

RETRO WOMAN

20 Pembridge Road, Notting Hill Gate W11 3HL
0207 565 5572
www.mgeshops.com
Mon-Sun 10:00-20:00
Notting Hill Gate Tube

Of all the London shops in the Music and Goods Exchange empire (encompassing secondhand music, clothing, homeware and book outlets, most of them in Notting Hill Gate), Retro Woman at 20 Pembridge Road has the most upmarket stock. Designer labels abound. The huge collection of shoes, from D&G, Fendi, Stella McCartney, Roberto Cavalli, Balenciaga and co, cries out for a red carpet to tread. On the racks, the clothes are modern designer vintage, from the likes of Gucci, Helmut Lang, Alexander McQueen and Lacroix. Designer sunglasses, bags and belts also feature. Err on the side of abandon and take plenty of cash. A sister shop, a few doors down, sells cheaper women's clothes.

●●£

ROKIT

42 Shelton Street, Covent Garden WC2H 9HZ
0207 836 6547
www.rokit.co.uk
Mon-Sat 10:00-19:00; Sun 11:00-18:00
Covent Garden Tube

Forget riffling through tubs of
unidentified clobber, Rokit is at
the meticulously organised end of
secondhand clothing. Much of the garb
here is modern American vintage, born
in the 1970s and 80s, although older, rarer
items can also be found if you've got
the time to search the racks, alongside
new hats, bags and other accessories.
The condition of the clothes is always
good, the prices unapologetic. Two other
shops in Brick Lane and one in Camden
complete Rokit's London line-up.

£££

ROWAN AND ROWAN

315 Grays Antique Market, 58 Davies Street,
Mayfair W1K 5LP
0207 629 7234
www.rowanandrowan.com
Mon, Wed, Fri 10:00-17:00
Bond Street Tube

All secondhand goods have a past life, but
at Rowan and Rowan the jewellery has
more history than most. The West End
shop sells antique jewellery dating back as
far as 1450. From the Georgian lovers' eye
miniatures to the memento mori skulls
and 18th century paste jewellery, the
contents are fascinating and unique, a fact
duly reflected in the prices. Michele, the
proprietor, has given lectures on antique
jewellery to the Friends of the V&A.

282

'We sell recycled skin'

CLAUDIA, 282

£ £ £ - £ £ £

282 Portobello Road, Notting Hill W10 5TE
Tue-Sun 12:00-17:00
07984 867799
Ladbroke Grove Tube

Entering 282 Portobello Road is an unusually sensory experience. The smell, of aged leather and waxed coats, hits you like a damp country show. Visually, there are lots of weathered browns, faded blacks and racing greens, whilst the textures of leather and fur add a certain tactile appeal. "We sell recycled skin," says Claudia, co-owner, cutting to the chase. "We specialise in quality English vintage; classic clothing, footwear and accessories. Some of it dates from the turn of the last century, but really you shouldn't be able to tell exactly when it dates from, because it's timeless, it's beyond fashion." The fur coats, riding boots, leather bags, tweed jackets and Barbour coats do indeed transcend the decades. Other items, from old flight bags to frocks, are more easily dated. In common, the garments are all lovingly preserved.

295

295 Portobello Road, Notting Hill W10 5TD
Fri-Sat 8.30-17:00
Ladbroke Grove Tube

The oldest vintage clothing shop on Portobello Road is also one of the cheapest. It's a den of a place, the dark walls lined with racks of clothes, the ceiling masked by an old cargo parachute. Most of the clothes date from the 1970s; anything older gets snapped up quickly. Few carry any label of note, but they're in universally good condition. The menswear section is unusually good, embracing everything from frock coats, to tweed jackets, bowties to cufflinks. A counter at the back of the shop gathers together vintage underwear and jewellery.

VINTAGE MODES

Grays Antiques Market, 1-7 Davies Mews,
Mayfair W1K 5AB
0207 629 7034
www.vintagemodes.co.uk
Mon-Fri 10:00-18:00
Bond Street Tube

Three traders sell their clothes from within the plush red, boudoir-like den of Vintage Modes, resident in the basement of Davies Mews. In common, the clothes, shoes and accessories are 'genuine' vintage; antique even, some dating back to the late Victorian period. Quality and authenticity pervade, attracting film and theatre costume researchers and fashion students alike. It's the place for a 1930s ballet tutu, a strapless lace brassiere or a showy YSL 80s belt. Vintage Modes also has extensive collections of fur, silk scarves and handbags.

🪙🪙£-🪙🪙🪙

THE VINTAGE SHOWROOM

14 Earlham Street, Seven Dials WC2H 9LN
0207 836 3964
www.thevintageshowroom.com
Mon-Sat 11:30-19:30; Sun 12:00-17:00
Covent Garden Tube

The men's clothes and accessories in the Vintage Showroom embalm mid 20th century style, and the prices duly reflect their heritage. Duffles, Letterman jackets, work-worn denim, cable knits and army dead stock fill the rails. Bang on for that Dylan Thomas look.

🪙🪙£

ABSOLUTE VINTAGE

15 Hanbury Street, Shoreditch E1 6QR
0207 247 3883
www.absolutevintage.co.uk
Mon-Sun 11:00-19:00
Liverpool Street/Aldgate East Tube

Simply put, the largest vintage shoe collection in the country, with footwear dating from the 1940s to the 90s and arranged by size. The range is astonishing and the prices are good. The shop has a warehouse feel – twee vintage boutique it isn't – and also stocks a good, selective range of clothes and accessories for women and men.

©£€-©£€

ANDREW
R ULLMANN LTD

36 Greville Street, London EC1N 8TB
0207 405 1877
www.arullmann.com
Mon-Sat 10:00-17:00
Farringdon Tube

This family firm has been part of the
Hatton Garden jewellery district since the
1950s; an earlier incarnation opened in
Budapest in 1902. The shop deals mainly
in antique and vintage jewellery, but also
has an intriguing collection of silver,
objects and oddities, from hip flasks to
vesta cases. The prices – ranging from £5
to £15,000 – reflect this variety.

©£€

ANTIQUE WATCH CO

19 Clerkenwell Road EC1M 5RS
0207 250 3734
www.antiquewatchcouk.com
Mon-Fri 11:00-16:30
Farringdon Tube

A small, quiet shop on a loud road, the
Antique Watch Co repairs and sells
antique and vintage wrist and pocket
watches. Many of the wristwatches date
back to the 1950s and 60s, their straps in
leather, their faces marked by the likes of
Omega, Breitling and Rolex. Much newer
watches, from Tag Heuer, Gucci and
others, are also sold.

CLERKENWELL VINTAGE FASHION FAIR

£££-£££

**The Old Finsbury Town Hall,
Rosebury Avenue EC1R 4RP
www.clerkenwellvintagefashionfair.co.uk
8 fairs a year on Sundays, £4 entry**

"Labels are important in vintage. Daywear and eveningwear by a known designer from the 1940s – that's vintage. Generally, I would describe a dress from the 1980s as secondhand." Savitri, creator of the Clerkenwell Vintage Fashion Fair, is explaining the nuances of vintage and secondhand. Tired of schlepping up West from her home in East London to find good vintage fashion fairs, she started her own, in Clerkenwell. Its setting, in the lavish art nouveau heart of Old Finsbury Town Hall, is perfect. The majority of the traders, drawn from as far as New York, sell clothes, from the 1800s through to the 1980s. Others specialise in hats, or concentrate on jewellery, textiles, handbags and even objet d'art. Most of the clothes are women's, although three or four stalls cater for men (a symptom, Savitri suggests, of the fact that men hold onto their clothes much longer than women). The prices here reflect the quality and age of the garments – all of which generates the sense that you're buying a lot more than simply something to wear.

●●£
DIRTY BLONDE

66A Cheshire Street, Shoreditch E2 6EH
0207 033 0282
www.styledgeneration.co.uk
Thu-Sun 11:00-18:00
Shoreditch High Street Overground

One of the Cheshire Street vintage
multitude (there are more vintage
clothing shops in this part of the East
End than anywhere else in London), Dirty
Blonde distinguishes herself with belts,
bags, shoes and a distinct 'East London'
feel. The shop eschews the 'rummage'
approach with well-spaced rails of hand-
picked women's clothes, all in very good
condition. A sister shop on Church Street,
Stoke Newington, also sells men's vintage
and more in the way of designer labels.

●●£
HIRSCHFELDS

Suite 26, 88-90 Hatton Garden EC1N 8TE
0207 405 1536
www.hirschfelds.co.uk
Mon-Fri 8:00-17:00
Farringdon Tube

Few of the Hatton Garden jewellers
have more history behind them than
Hirschfelds. They've been here since 1875.
Much of the secondhand stock is antique
(some of it recently salvaged from an
1860s shipwreck) but Hirschfelds also
has an impressive array of vintage jewels,
from delicate Art Deco brooches to the
oversized rings of the 1950s and 60s.

HUNKY DORY

226 Brick Lane, Shoreditch E1 6SA
0207 729 7387
www.hunkydoryvintage.com
Mon-Sun 11:30-18:30
Shoreditch High Street Overground

The charming old wooden frontage of Hunky Dory invites you into a small shop selling expertly edited vintage clothes for both men and women. The stock of shirts and dresses from the 1960s is particularly strong, but perhaps the biggest draw (for men at least) is the rack of kempt three-piece suits down in the basement, some dating back to the 40s. If you've ever wondered where Jarvis Cocker buys those sleek 70s ensembles, wonder no more.

Levisons

'We try and hand pick the mainly British clothes that we think people want'

MICHAEL, LEVISONS

£££-£££

1 Cheshire Street, Shoreditch E2 6ED
07762 793273
Mon-Sun; 12:00 until late
Shoreditch High Street Overground

Michael Levison's small but well stocked Shoreditch shop majors on good men's secondhand clothing. Indeed, amongst the multitude of London shops professing to sell genuine 'vintage', Levisons stakes a more valid claim than many. With immaculate tan brogues, spotless suits dating back to the 1940s, silk scarves and tweed hats, much of the stock is the real deal, although the racks also feature less pedigreed items, not least some colourful 1980s jumpers. "We try and hand pick the mainly British clothes that we think people want," says Michael, pointing out an original Belstaff wax cotton coat as evidence. In common, all the clothes are pristinely presented – no stale fug in the air here. Michael also stocks a selection of women's vintage clothing, along with an interesting collection of aging travel cases.

PAPER
DRESS

114-116 Curtain Road, Shoreditch EC2A 3AH
0207 729 4100
www.paperdressvintage.co.uk
Mon-Sat 10:30-19:30; Sun 12:00-18:00
Shoreditch High Street Overground
Old Street Tube

Being a few streets removed from the secondhand and vintage hub of Brick Lane has prompted Hannah, proprietor of Paper Dress, to think laterally. She's turned an unremarkable 1980s Shoreditch shop space into a boho haven. It centres on vintage clothing but spirals out to include much more besides. Having a coffee shop in amongst the rails is genius. It gives Paper Dress an immediate sociability, offering up a comfy chair in which to slump whilst Hannah works on your clothes (she offers an alteration service), or on which to park the boyfriend with a chocolate muffin whilst you browse.

Regular events (or 'Paper Dresstivals') in the shop feature bands, DJs, dancers and discounts on the clothes. A license to sell alcohol eases the evening events snugly into an area renowned for its nightlife. As for the gear, Paper Dress stocks a varied mix of genuine vintage and more modern gear for women and men, including clothes, shoes (loads), belts and hats. A few pieces of old electronica – radios, record players and telephones – hide amongst the clothes.

SKEWIFF AND SCATTY

€ £ £

64 Sclater Street, Shoreditch E1 6HR
Thu-Sun, mid-morning until late
Shoreditch High Street Overground

Pickles, as exuberant as her name implies, has been selling secondhand goods around London for 30 years. "I'm a recycler," she explains. "Have been all my life. I like to alter things; to take old clothes and renew them." Her latest shop sits amongst Sclater Street's railway arches, recently refreshed as part of the East London Line revamp. The stock is well chosen, the premises' lack of space ensuring that items are selected on merit. Costume jewellery is a speciality but the shop is also crammed with bags, hats, ceramics, purses, rag dolls, framed pictures, tea trays and other domestic detritus. The clothes are cheap and largely cheerful, although sustained rummaging might turn up a genuine vintage piece.

'I like to alter things; to take old clothes and renew them'

PICKLES, SKEWIFF AND SCATTY

THE VINTAGE EMPORIUM

14 Bacon Street, Shoreditch E1 6LF
0207 739 0799
www.vintageemporiumcafe.com
Mon-Sun 10:00-19:00 (café 10:00-22:00)
Shoreditch High Street Overground

Each of the vintage shops on and around
Brick Lane has its own personality, its
own twist on selling secondhand clothes.
At The Vintage Emporium the large
basement of clothes, with its discerning
collection of genuine vintage garb, hats,
luggage and other accessories dating
from the Victorian period through to
the rationing years, is combined with a
terrific tearoom above and – surely
unique amongst the vintage shopping
fellowship – life drawing, drama and
open mic evenings.

ANNIE'S

12 Camden Passage, Islington N1 8ED
0207 359 0796
www.anniesvintageclothing.co.uk
Mon-Sun 11:00-18:00
Angel Tube

Annie's, a long-time resident of Camden Passage, has some of the oldest clothes on sale in London. Indeed, many of the garments and fabrics here are antique, even whilst the majority date from the 1920s to the 40s. Silk, fur and lace predominate. The flapper dresses, shawls, fur capes, wedding veils and lacy petticoats have attracted the likes of Kate Moss, Ralph Lauren and Donna Karan.

CAMDEN VINTAGE

Unit D10/11 Horse Tunnel Market,
Chalk Farm Road, Camden NW1 8AH
07767 714213
Mon-Sun 11:00-18:00
Chalk Farm/Camden Town Tube

Camden Vintage focuses its attention on a select clique of clothing brands and styles and then packs the rail with those particular items. So, they've got a remarkable stock of both single and double breasted Burberry coats from the 1950s to the 70s (the days when they were made in the UK), alongside rows of Barbour jackets, Aran knits, American Levi's and other fashion icons. It's also the place to go for a genuine 1930s top hat and tails, or a secondhand Queen's Guard uniform.

Vintage
CLOTHING
FAIRS

The surge of interest in vintage clothing and accessories
has spawned a number of vintage fashion fairs in London.
They tend to be vintage distilled, the stallholders compelled
by the limitations of space into only taking the best, most
genuine vintage clothing, jewellery and bags that you'll find
in the capital. Most occur once a month, although some take
a brief summer break. Keep an eye on *Time Out London*
and other local press for forthcoming dates.

JUDY'S AFFORDABLE VINTAGE FAIR

www.vintagefair.co.uk

A national operation that turns up in East London about once a month. Venues have included York Hall in Bethnal Green and Spitalfields Old Market.

THE VINTAGE FAIR

www.thevintagefair.com

Another touring affair that puts down in East London, taking up temporary residence every couple of months in Shoreditch Town Hall or Hanbury Hall, just off Brick Lane.

PRIMROSE HILL VINTAGE FASHION FAIR

www.vintagefashionfairlondon.co.uk

A relaxed Sunday affair held roughly once a month in Cecil Sharp House on Regents Park Road.

ANITA'S VINTAGE FASHION FAIRS

www.vintagefashionfairs.com

Regular events interchange between Battersea Arts Centre and Notting Hill's 20th Century Theatre.

NORTH LONDON VINTAGE MARKET

www.northlondonvintagemarket.co.uk

Furniture, books and homeware are also included in bi-monthly fairs at St Mary's Parish Hall in Crouch End or Stoke Newington Library Gallery.

FROCK ME

www.frockmevintagefashion.com

Amongst the first and most popular of London's vintage clothing fairs, Frock Me takes up a Sunday residence in Chelsea Town Hall roughly once a month.

CLERKENWELL VINTAGE FASHION FAIR

www.clerkenwellvintagefashionfair.co.uk

Held eight times a year in the wonderful surrounds of The Old Finsbury Town Hall.

HAMMERSMITH VINTAGE FAIR

www.pa-antiques.co.uk

A monthly regular at Hammersmith Town Hall for the last decade, and which, on occasion, morphs into a Vintage Bridal Fair.

CAMDEN THRIFT STORE

51 Chalk Farm Road, Camden NW1 8AN
Mon-Sun 12:30-18:30
Chalk Farm Tube

Camden Thrift Store is a student of the pile 'em high school, stuffed with all manner of secondhand clothes and accessories. The prices are disarmingly cheap and the proprietor, Lyn, irrepressibly enthusiastic. Countless visitors have no doubt stepped inside to escape the Camden rain and left with a 1970s wedding dress, a fine rabbit fur cape from the 40s or a purple wig. Lyn offers an adjustment service, and readily acknowledges the rather indiscriminate range of the shop, serving as it does everyone from fancy-dress partygoer to fashionista.

CRISTOBAL

€€€-€€€

26 Church Street, Marylebone NW8 8EP
0207 724 7230
www.cristobal.co.uk
Tue-Sat 10:30-16:30
Marylebone/Edgware Road Tube

The contents of Cristobal reflect the
shop's eclectic ethos. Period costume
jewellery lines up alongside antique and
mid 20th century furniture and lighting;
some of it decorative, some of it industrial.

A DANDY IN ASPIC

€€€

Unit D13 Horse Tunnel Market and Unit 566
Stables Market, both off Chalk Farm Road,
Camden NW1 8AH
0207 485 3979
Mon-Fri 11:00-18:30; Sat-Sun 10:00-19:00
Chalk Farm/Camden Town Tube

Given the small size of its two shops – one
solely menswear (Stables Market), the
other men's and women's (Horse Tunnel
Market) – A Dandy in Aspic packs quite
a punch. The clothes are top end vintage,
hand picked, lovingly presented and well
preserved. Silk scarves, panamas, brogues
– the shops have a taste for classic style
with a Mod element thrown in. "It's
not just about the clothes, it's about a
whole lifestyle," goes the Dandy in Aspic
philosophy. Buy the clothes
and look sharp.

GENERAL EYEWEAR

**Arch 67, Stables Market, Chalk Farm Road,
Camden NW1 8AH
0207 428 0123
www.archiv.net
Tue-Thu 12:00-18:00; Sat-Sun 10:00-18:00
Chalk Farm/Camden Town Tube**

A rather broad name for what is a singular
shop, General Eyewear sells frames and
sunglasses dating back as far as 200
years. The cabinets and drawers of the
atmospheric Camden Stables outfit,
shared with Archiv menswear, harbour
original classics, but of equal interest is
the shop's bespoke service. Using original
pattern sheets, catalogues and materials
they can make 'new' vintage specs to fit
your very own face. As worn by Beyoncé,
Elton John and Willy Wonka (aka
Johnny Depp).

21ST CENTURY RETRO

**162 Holloway Road, Holloway N7 8DD
0207 700 2354
www.londonvintagestore.com
Mon-Sat 10:00-18:00; Sun 11:00-18:00
Holloway Road Tube**

Tardis-esque, its small, unnamed facade
belying the long shop behind, the 21st
Century Retro store has rack after rack
of men's and women's clothes, shoes and
accessories from the 1940s through to the
90s. The approach is 'warehouse' even if
the premises aren't, and the clothes are
correspondingly good value.

ⓐⓑⓒ-ⓐⓑⓒ

OLD HAT VINTAGE

66 Fulham High Street, SW6 3LQ
0207 610 6558
Mon-Sat 10:30-18:30
Putney Bridge Tube

A celebration of classic men's tailoring, Old Hat sells secondhand tweeds, Savile Row suits, waistcoats and dinner jackets, and has done for some time. Most of the evening and daywear is from the 1950s to 70s, and has the attendant quality you'd expect. The fact that owner Dave Saxby, an aficionado of the classic English look, has another shop in Tokyo confirms that this kind of gear is both timeless and borderless, ungoverned by the whims of fashion.

ⓐⓑⓒ-ⓐⓑⓒ

RETROMANIA

6 Upper Tachbrook Street,
Pimlico SW1V 1SH
0207 630 7406
www.faracharityshops.org
Mon-Sat 10:00-18:00; Sun 11:00-17:00
Victoria Tube

Retromania is a weightier outfit than the daft name might suggest. It's run by FARA, a charity with a string of shops, but the contents are far more select than the charity shop norm. Many of the clothes, shoes and accessories here are designer, from the likes of Chloe wedges to a 1960s Peggy French coat or a 1969 Biba lace dress, and some are genuine period pieces, like the satin lace wedding dress from the 1920s. They're not perfect; indeed, some look worn (no surprise given their age). Most of the contents are for gals, although boys do a get a couple of racks and some shoes. Downstairs, the 'Sale Basement' has more prosaic, affordable clothes.

EMPORIUM

330-332 Creek Road, Greenwich SE10 9SW
0208 305 1670
Wed-Sun 10:30-18:00
Cutty Sark DLR

The majority of London's vintage clothing shops have appeared in the last ten years. Emporium, however, has been a Greenwich fixture for a quarter of a century. The reassuring wisdom of that lifespan resonates in the women's and men's clothes and accessories on sale. Owners Jonathan and Jacqueline understand the value of one-off vintage wear, whether it's dead stock Christian Dior sunglasses, red tag Levi's or a Savile Row suit. Emporium has an eye for good British tailoring, something that has drawn numerous fashion designers and film stylists to the shop over the years (Tom Cruise's *Mission Impossible* leather jacket came from here). From 1950s ball gowns to 60s mod jackets, the clothes are immaculately presented. Silk scarves, hats and jewellery are also in abundance.

87 Lower Marsh, Waterloo SE1 7AB
0207 928 0800
www.radiodaysvintage.co.uk
Mon-Sat 10:00-18:00
Waterloo/Lambeth North Tube

RADIO DAYS

At Radio Days you can see how the different elements of vintage knit together. How, for the passionate, nostalgia can become a lifestyle choice. Or, you can dip in and out, picking the elements you like, whether that's a knee-length 1970s leather Mac, a piece of Poole pottery from the 50s or an old Woodbines box. "Some people wear vintage clothes – and only vintage clothes – every day of the week," confirms Lee, who runs with the shop with co-owner, Chrissie. "Other people come to the shop because they're sourcing genuine items for a drama piece." It's a remarkable collection of clothes and collectibles, from handbags to jewellery, telephones to books (including a fine selection of genuine 60s pulp fiction). The hat selection – trilbies, fedoras, pork pies, bowlers, caps (and that's just the men's) – is particularly choice.

'Some people wear vintage clothes – and only vintage clothes – every day of the week'

LEE, RADIO DAYS

UMI AND CO VINTAGE

320-322 Creek Road, Greenwich SE10 9SW
0208 858 1964
www.umiandco.com
Tue-Fri 10:30-18:00; Sat 10:30-18:30;
Sun 12:00-18:00
Cutty Sark DLR

Sharing its premises with Casbah Records
(see chapter two), Umi is a diminutive
vintage clothes and accessories shop.
The small scale means there aren't piles
of clothes to fight through, and also that
what is here is carefully selected. Much of
the contents, for men and women, dates
from the 1950s and 60s, although some
of the dresses are pre-war. A few bits of
homeware, including lamps and the like,
add to the nostalgic glow.

WHAT THE BUTLER WORE

131 Lower Marsh, Waterloo SE1 7AE
0207 261 1353
www.whatthebutlerwore.co.uk
Mon-Sat 11:00-18:00
Waterloo/Lambeth North Tube

The care, attention and love for the
clothes in What The Butler Wore are
immediately apparent. Each item, as
befits an Ossie Clark dress or a 60s
mohair pencil skirt, is given due
reverence. Most of the clothes, bags
and shoes here date from the 1960s and
70s, although earlier items can also be
found. As co-owner Bridget explains,
"We try and sell clothes that people can
work into their modern wardrobe or, if
they want, wear as a complete vintage
ensemble." Slightly removed from the
main tourist routes, in the shadow of
Waterloo, the prices are good too.

BOOKS, MUSIC & MEMORABILIA

Vinyl / Cameras / Posters
Books and Magazines
CDs and DVDs / Coins
Musical Instruments

BOB DYLAN

JIMI HENDRIX

THE SMITHS

METALLICA

CERTAIN THINGS RISE SERENELY ABOVE THE VAGARIES OF FASHION. A VINYL COPY OF *BEATLES FOR SALE*, A GIBSON LES PAUL GUITAR, THE NOVELS OF DICKENS (WHO, INCIDENTALLY, WROTE ABOUT LONDON'S SECONDHAND SHOPS IN HIS *SKETCHES BY BOZ*) OR A MODEL STARS WARS AT-AT WALKER – ALL HAVE AN INTRINSIC VALUE, HOWEVER OLD OR UNLOVED THEY MAY HAVE BECOME. INDEED, CULTURE IS AS GOOD SECONDHAND AS IT IS NEW.

Many of London's secondhand book, music, instrument and toy shops, packed with this cultural appeal, call out to the casual browser. The contents can be fascinating but inexpensive; the goods regularly recycled. That well thumbed copy of *Catch 22*, for example, could easily find its way to a different secondhand bookshop within six months.

Meanwhile, other shops cater to the collector, selling coveted and expensive rarities, be they comics, coins or posters. And London is sufficiently big to do the specifics incredibly well. Where else will you find a store selling only accordions? Or a bookshop concerned solely with secondhand children's literature? Often, the experts huddle together. As in Cecil Court or Bloomsbury with its bookshops, or in Denmark Street, aka Tin Pan Alley, still going strong as a hub for secondhand musical instruments.

ADRIAN HARRINGTON RARE BOOKS

64a Kensington Church Street, Kensington W8 4DB
0207 937 1465
www.harringtonbooks.co.uk
Mon-Sat 11:00-17:00
Kensington High Street/ Notting Hill Gate Tube

The location of Adrian Harrington Rare Books, amidst the cultured antique shops of Kensington Church Street, hints at its eminence, and inside the shelves are duly filled with rare first editions and bound library sets in all genres. Rows of old Dickens, Conan Doyle and Austen live alongside more recent books, music memorabilia and film posters (including original adverts for Hammer Horror, *Get Carter* and the like). There's a particularly good collection of Churchilliana, much of it autographed by Sir Winston himself. The shop also stocks the oldest of old books, usually tucked away from public view – the likes of Nostradamus' *Prophecies*, printed circa 1670.

APERTURE CAMERA CAFÉ

44 Museum Street, Holborn WC1A 1LY
0207 242 8681
www.apertureuk.com
Mon-Fri 11:00-19:00; Sat 12:00-19:00
Holborn/Tottenham Court Road Tube

Surely any shop is improved by the addition of a café. Browsing the many and varied secondhand cameras in this charming camera specialists, the knowledge that a steaming Americano awaits you at a table nearby lifts the experience markedly. In particular, the Aperture Camera Café sells Cannon Autofocus, Nikon Manual and Autofocus, Hasselblad and medium format rangefinder cameras. They're convinced that 35mm film has a role to play in the digital age. "People like the tactility," they explain. "And, if you're using film you really have to think before you shoot. You haven't got an 8mg memory card with hundreds of photos on it; you have film, and each shot costs money – so you really think about the composition, the light, what you're shooting." And for all of which, you need a shot of caffeine.

🪙£ £

BOOK AND COMIC EXCHANGE

14 Pembridge Road,
Notting Hill Gate W11 3HT
0207 229 8420
www.mgeshops.com
Mon-Sun 10:00-20:00
Notting Hill Gate Tube

The literary wing of the Music and Video Exchange chain of Notting Hill shops has many of the essential qualities of a good a secondhand bookshop: slightly scruffy, mildly claustrophobic and packed with cheapish books. The crime, mystery and thrillers section is extensive, as are the shelves devoted to horror, history and biography. A central aisle harbours numerous cheap comics, as well as a few more collectible pieces and old copies of *Vogue* and *Record Collector*. The Sci-fi corridor speaks for itself whilst the extensive basement has thousands of books selling for 50p.

🪙🪙£

CAMERA CITY

16 Little Russell Street, Holborn WC1A 2HL
0207 813 2100
www.cameracity.co.uk
Mon-Fri 10:00-17:30; Sat 10:30-14:00
Holborn/Tottenham Court Road Tube

Small, unassuming and knowledgeable, Camera City serves a broad church of photographers. They sell secondhand cameras of all makes, rank and age (including the digital age), from Hassleblad to Nikon, and will also take your old camera in part exchange. Accessories, repairs and camera servicing are also available.

CEX

32 Rathbone Place, Fitzrovia W1T 1JJ
0845 345 1664
uk.webuy.com
Mon-Wed and Sat, 10:00-19:30; Thu-Fri
10:00-20:00; Sun 11:00-19:00
Tottenham Court Road Tube

Most of the shops in the Complete
Entertainment Exchange (CEX) empire
sell electronics of all breeds, from iPads
to mobile phones and plasma TVs, but the
rather dishevelled Rathbone Place store
majors on secondhand video games. The
choice isn't boundless but it's not bad,
and the prices seem fair (for both
buyers and sellers).

THE CLASSIC CAMERA

2 Pied Bull Yard (off Bury Place),
Holborn WC1A 2JR
0207 831 0777
www.theclassiccamera.com
Mon-Fri 9:45-17:30; Sat 10:00-16:30
Holborn/Tottenham Court Road Tube

Situated in what could be called London's
secondhand camera district – the lanes
and squares leading off Great Russell
Street opposite the British Museum –
The Classic Camera displays its German
optics (they specialise in Voigtländer,
Zeiss and Leica) with due reverence; the
likes of a 1920 Leica Rim-Set Compur, on
sale for £4,000, has earned its place in
the glass cabinet. Expect friendly staff,
expertise and impeccably presented
cameras. They also service old Leicas
and sell new models.

CLASSICAL MUSIC EXCHANGE

36 Notting Hill Gate, Notting Hill W11 3HX
0207 229 3219
www.mgeshops.com
Mon-Sun 10:00-20:00
Notting Hill Gate Tube

This densely stocked Notting Hill Gate shop is almost unique amongst London's secondhand music shops in its insistence on selling only classical music, be it in vinyl (33s, 45s, 78s and box sets), tape, CD, DVD or laser disc form. It's a brilliant shop, undiscriminating in its content, with classical vinyl that ranges in price from a few pence (at least half of the albums sell for less than £1) to hundreds of pounds. Neil, a font of knowledge behind the counter, will help your search. A basement room is packed with the cheapest of the secondhand vinyl, whilst a mezzanine upstairs harbours the shop's only deviation from classical music – shelves of cheap secondhand books.

COINCRAFT

44 & 45 Great Russell Street, WC1B 3LU
0207 636 1188
www.coincraft.com
Mon-Fri 9:30-17:00; Sat 10:00-14:30
Russell Square Tube

For more than 50 years Coincraft has been selling coins, banknotes and assorted antiquities of the sort that evoke the contents of its near neighbour, the British Museum. From a miniature terracotta horse dating from Antiquity, or a 1,700-year-old Roman coin, to a 2002 £5 note, withdrawn from circulation because the serial number was defective, the shops (it's actually two premises side by side) sell all manner of collectibles (and boast the largest stock of coins and banknotes in the UK). The enthusiasm of the staff, evidently smitten with their stock, is infectious.

ⓢⓕⓕ-ⓢⓕⓕ
COLIN NARBUTH AND SONS

20 Cecil Court,
off Charing Cross Road WC2N 4HE
0207 379 6975
www.colin-narbeth.com
Tue-Fri 10:30-17:30;
Mon and Sat 10.30-16:00
Leicester Square Tube

A small shop packed with old bank notes, cigarette cards, medals and other military memorabilia. Some of the stock is extremely rare, such as a first issue John Bradbury £1 note from 1914; some taps into popular culture – as in the collection of Beatles cigarette cards. The crates of charming old postcards, sold cheaply, have a habit of sucking you in, whilst the Nazi documents on the wall behind the counter hold a more sombre fascination.

ⓢⓕⓕ
GAY'S THE WORD

66 Marchmont Street, Bloomsbury WC1N 1AB
0207 278 7654
www.gaystheword.co.uk
Mon-Sat 10:00-18:30; Sun 14:00-16:00
Russell Square Tube

The first (and now sole surviving) gay and lesbian bookshop in Britain, Gay's the Word is something of a Bloomsbury institution. Three quarters of the books here are new, but the goodly section of secondhand stock contains out of print, rare and not so rare titles. Some are profound (*Sexual Orientation and Human Rights*), others less so (*The Ultimate Guide to Fellatio*). With regular book readings and other social events, Gay's the Word operates as a community hub as well as a bookshop.

HOBGOBLIN MUSIC

24 Rathbone Place, Fitzrovia W1T 1JA
0207 323 9040
www.hobgoblin.com
Mon-Sat 10:00-18:00
Tottenham Court Road/Goodge Street Tube

The Hobgoblin shop just off Oxford Street, one of a small chain of outlets around the UK, sells a good stock of secondhand instruments from the folkier end of the musical spectrum. It's a varied mix of new stuff, weird and wonderful collectibles and more workaday modern secondhand instruments. Squeezeboxes, acoustic guitars, mandolins and harps rub shoulders with more exotic items – would you know a 200-year-old Nepalese Shamanic drum if you heard one? The staff are happy to offer enlightenment.

INTOXICA

231 Portobello Road, Notting Hill W11 1LT
0207 229 8010
www.intoxica.co.uk
Mon-Sat 10:30-18:30; Sun 12noon-5pm
Ladbroke Grove Tube

Most of the treasures that set Intoxica, Portobello's prime secondhand record shop, apart from the crowd lie downstairs, where a jazz collection best described as 'left of centre' serves up old Charlie Mingus, Herbie Mann and Thelonious Monk discs. Prices vary markedly depending on collectibility. At street level the selection is more soul, pop and rock led. Whilst the shop only sells music in vinyl form, it does also have vintage film posters and a select shelf or two of secondhand music books.

MARCHPANE

16 Cecil Court, off Charing Cross Road
WC2N 4HE
0207 836 8661
www.marchpane.com
Mon-Sat 11:00-18:00
Leicester Square Tube

Marchpane specialises in children's and illustrated books. The small shop is crammed with titles from the authors that have sent children off to sleep for generations, from AA Milne to JK Rowling. The books here are collector's items. It's the place to go for a Heath Robinson-illustrated copy of Hans Christian Andersen's *Fairy Tales*, or a first edition of *Peter and Wendy*. Try not to be put off by the multiple instructional signs on how to handle the books.

A PLACE IN SPACE

237 Shaftesbury Avenue WC2H 8EH
0207 836 5630
Mon-Wed 10:30-18:30;
Thu-Sat 10:00-19:00; Sun 10:00-16:00
Tottenham Court Road Tube

Stepping into A Place in Space at the busy junction of New Oxford Street and Shaftesbury Avenue there's a reverent hush amid the row upon row of comics and graphic novels. It's everything a good comic shop should be. No frills, just comics, and with staff who know their stuff. A Place in Space specialise in silver, golden age and bronze age comics, spanning the second half of the 20th century, sold alongside new editions and collectible toys. Prices vary accordingly.

OXFAM BLOOMSBURY

12 Bloomsbury Street WC1B 3QA
0207 637 4610
oxfambloomsburybooks.wordpress.com
Mon-Sat 10:00-18:00; Sun 12:00-17:00
Tottenham Court Road Tube

Oxfam's principal secondhand bookstore in London, just around the corner from the British Museum, is a neat, well-ordered affair with consistently good stock. If you're looking for a contemporary author, particularly in fiction, you're likely to find their work here, sold at a decent price. The shop also hosts intermittent poetry readings and book signings.

R.G. GRAHAME

129/130 Grays Antique Market,
28 Davies Street, Mayfair W1K 5LP
07969 444239
Mon-Fri 11:00-17:00
Bond Street Tube

Gordon's shop in the basement of Grays Antique Market reminds us how we used to see the world; through grainy lithographs, black and white magazines, intricate maps or hand-coloured prints. Some of the mounted pictures here date back to the 17th century, such as a print of John Bunyan, ruddy-faced even in black and white. More recent works include *Winnie the Pooh* prints from the 1930s and hand-coloured lithographs of Alfred Hitchcock and others by *The New York Times* caricaturist Al Hirschfeld. Given their age, the items are reasonably priced.

R.G. LEWIS

29 Southampton Row, Holborn WC1B 5HL
0207 242 2916
www.rglewis.co.uk
Mon-Thu 8:30-17:00; Fri 8:30-17:00;
Sat 9:30-15:45
Holborn Tube

Dating back to 1881, the R.G. Lewis business is as venerable as the secondhand Leica cameras it stocks. Indeed, go to Hong Kong or New York, ask about Leica cameras and, the R.G. Lewis staff assure, you'll be directed to the humble Holborn shop. The decor is utilitarian – the stock takes centre stage. The secondhand Leicas, some dating back 80 years or more, are sold alongside new models. The staff are experts in their field, whilst each secondhand camera sold comes with a six-month guarantee. Be warned—Leica collectors need to match their enthusiasm with deep pockets.

ON TIN PAN ALLEY

Various London streets found fame in the swinging Sixties: Carnaby Street, the King's Road and so on. But only Denmark Street, a short, shady but rousing Soho thoroughfare remains proficient in the field that made its name – music. Most of the buildings on Denmark Street date to the 19th century, an era when it built a reputation for publishing sheet music. By the 1930s the shops selling pianos and guitars had arrived and the road had been informally christened Tin Pan Alley. Then came the recording studios and the bands. The Rolling Stones recorded their first album in the Regent Sounds Studio, at 4 Denmark Street, in 1964. The Kinks, Stevie Wonder and Jimi Hendrix followed the Stones' lead. In the 70s The Clash and David Bowie would hang out at the Giaconda Café in between recording sessions. The Sex Pistols had a flat three doors down. Today, the street remains a magnet for music lovers, keen to soak up the mystique and to browse the gaggle of music shops, many selling secondhand instruments.

SAX

21 Denmark Street, Soho WC2H 8NA
0207 836 7172
www.sax.co.uk
Mon-Fri 10:00-18:00; Sat 10:00-17:00
Tottenham Court Road Tube

The vast majority of saxophones in Denmark Street's dedicated sax shop are new, but it's worth visiting for the half dozen or so vintage instruments that hang on the wall mid-shop, overlooking the young pretenders. Most are made by Selmer, and most are altos (the tenor Selmer saxophones that come in sell very quickly). Some date back to the 1930s and 40s, but more often they're of the later Mark VI variety. Each has a résumé listing former roles, be it as part of the Pasadena Roof Orchestra or on a Basement Jaxx recording.

SISTER RAY RECORDS

34-35 Berwick Street, Soho W1F 8RP
0207 734 3297
www.sisterray.co.uk
Mon-Sat 10:00-20:00; Sun 12:00-18:00
Tottenham Court Road/Oxford Circus Tube

A long-time resident in the heart of Soho's old (and fading) vinyl district, Sister Ray is an indie record shop selling mostly new CDs and vinyl, but with a good stock of collectible secondhand stuff too. It's darkish, loud and well organised (no overflowing crates here) – perfect for lazy, uninterrupted vinyl grazing. Mono pressings from the 60s – from *Revolver* to *Blonde on Blonde* – seem a speciality, although all vintages and genres are covered.

€££

SKOOB

**66 The Brunswick, off Marchmont Street,
Bloomsbury WC1N 1AE
0207 278 8760
www.skoob.com
Mon-Sat 10:30-20:00; Sun 10:30-18:00
Russell Square Tube**

Don't judge Skoob by its cover. The
entrance may be a banal shop front at the
northern end of the blocky Brunswick
Centre, a five-minute walk from Russell
Square, but step inside, go down the stairs,
and you'll find yourself in one of the best
secondhand bookshops in London. It's a
subterranean delight. Packed primarily
(but certainly not exclusively) with used
academic books, the shop reveals itself
slowly, its myriad sections tucked away
around shelves and corners. 'Marxism',
'Globalisation', 'Terrorism' read the more
cerebral section headings; others point
you towards fiction (not least a huge
collection of Penguin orange titles), art
books and audiobooks. An old piano
petitions you next to a shelf of music
books and a box of classical records.

SOUNDS OF THE UNIVERSE

7 Broadwick Street, Soho W1F 0DA
0207 734 3430
www.soundsoftheuniverse.com
Mon-Sat 11:00-19:30
Tottenham Court Road/Oxford Circus Tube

With its own label (Soul Jazz Records) and a lot of new stock, Sounds of the Universe can afford to be selective about its secondhand vinyl. They don't do mainstream. Instead reggae, disco, funk, soul, Latin and world beats take precedence. A lot of it's rare and all of it's in good condition. Most of the secondhand stuff is in the basement. The shop itself is housed in a fantastic old building, a former boozer clad in toffee-glaze tiles.

STAGE & SCREEN

34 Notting Hill Gate, Notting Hill W11 3HX
0207 460 6716
www.mgeshops.com
Mon-Sun 10:00-20:00
Notting Hill Gate Tube

There are precious few secondhand film shops left in London. Downloads and mail orders have stolen their thunder. Notting Hill's Stage and Screen shop is a rare survivor; intact in part, no doubt, because of the sheer breadth of DVDs it sells. From *Steptoe and Son* to *Zombieland*, all filmic life is here under one roof. TV series box sets are also in abundance. Notes on the DVD spines comment on the outward appearance of discs, although the staff hasn't the time to check each DVD plays perfectly (each is sold with guarantee).

TRAVIS AND EMERY

17 Cecil Court, off Charing Cross Road
WC2N 4EZ
0207 240 2129
www.travis-and-emery.com
Mon-Sat 10:15-18:45; Sun 11:30-16:30
Leicester Square Tube

Travis and Emery is a shop that flags up Cecil Court's unique appeal. Anywhere else, a bookshop specialising in secondhand music and music literature would be unlikely to survive, let alone prosper for 50 years. The variety of biographies on Handel, Stravinsky and the rest is impressive, but the shop is of most import for the breadth of musical scores on sale. There are shelves of opera scores and rows of music for piano, trombone, euphonium, cello, guitar and any other instrument you might play. All very apt given that Mozart lodged in Cecil Court, aged eight, in the midst of his 'Child Genius' European concert tour. The shop also sells a few secondhand classical CDs and music related prints.

BOOKISH CHARMS

Graham Greene's proclamation – "Thank God! Cecil Court remains Cecil Court" – is still apposite. The short, paved alleyway between Charing Cross Road and St Martin's Lane has been home to several antiquarian and rare booksellers since the early 20th century. The street was first laid out in the 17th century, and it remains in the hands of the Cecil family today, even while the current incarnation was built in the late Victorian period. After its 1890s revamp Cecil Court became known as 'Flicker Alley', as film distributors and the suppliers of early film equipment took up residence. However, the publishers and booksellers began to prevail after the First World War. Today, the row is home to various intriguing bookshops, such as theatre memorabilia specialist Pleasures of Times Past, and Goldsboro Books, with their vast collection of signed first editions.

VINTAGE MAGAZINE SHOP

39-43 Brewer Street, Soho W1F 9UD
0207 439 8525
www.vinmag.com
Mon-Wed 10:00-19:00; Thu 10:00-20:00;
Fri-Sat 10:00-22:00; Sun 12:00-20:00
Piccadilly Circus Tube

The intrigue at the Vintage Magazine Shop in Soho resides downstairs, in a windowless basement stuffed with old magazines and newspapers. Given an hour or two, you could chart the course of modern western history down here, from the 1940s edition of *Picture Post* with young Princess Elizabeth on the cover to an *Evening Standard* dated September 11th 2001. Old and not so old editions of *Vogue*, *Playboy*, *Radio Times*, *Boxing Illustrated* and so on pack the shelves, arranged by decade. Most cost around £15, although expect to pay significantly more for rare editions, particularly those with a now dead, deified cover star. Old film posters and celeb autographs can also be had downstairs.

VINTAGE AND RARE GUITARS

6 Denmark Street, Soho WC2H 8LX
0207 240 7500
www.vintageandrareguitars.com
Mon-Sat 10:00-18:00; Sun 12:00-16:00
Tottenham Court Road Tube

The finest collection of vintage electric guitars on sale in London is in the heart of Tin Pan Alley as was. The instruments are iconic, from Gibson 335s, Les Pauls and Firebirds to Fender Strats and Teles and Rickenbacker basses. They hang on the walls like works of art. Ask nicely and they'll let you have a go on one. You might even bump into rock royalty: Paul Weller, Johnny Marr, Ray Davies and Chrissie Hynde have all been in.

⑤⑤£-⑤⑤£

DUKE OF UKE

22 Hanbury Street, Shoreditch E1 6QR
0207 247 7924
www.dukeofuke.co.uk
Tue-Fri 12:00-19:00; Sat-Sun 11:00-18:00
Liverpool Street/Aldgate East Tube

You can count London's ukulele and banjo emporiums on one finger; and this is it, the homely, much-loved Duke of Uke. Most of the instruments are new, but there is a select clique of secondhand standard and banjo ukes, hung on the wall next to the counter and displayed in a glass case. The oldest date back to the 1930s. Everyone here is an enthusiast; indeed, with gigs, tuition and a recording studio, the Duke of Uke bills itself as a community hub as much as a shop – perfectly in tune with the unassuming but newly fashionable uke itself.

SPITALFIELDS RECORD FAIR

£££-£££

Old Spitalfields Market, Spitalfields E1 6EW
First and third Friday of the month
10:30-16:30
Liverpool Street/Aldgate East Tube

A dozen or more stalls (nearly all manned by brilliantly knowledgeable middle aged blokes) appear at the bi-monthly record fair in Old Spitalfields Market. Most sell vinyl from across the genres, although punk and new wave seem particularly well represented. One stall specialises in 45s from the 1950s and 60s; another sells only CDs and box sets; and a third seems concerned solely with psychedelia. Alan, a former DJ, has been bringing his Dallysounds stall to Spitalfields for three years, selling all manner of vinyl, from reggae to Led Zeppelin. He says the fair attracts old and young alike: "I'm finding that the younger generation are really into vinyl. They like the depth of sound that you get from it; they like how tactile it is; and they like the artwork. They get things from vinyl that you can't necessarily get from an MP3 file or a CD. I think they also like the fact that it's something you have to care for." (See chapter four for more on Old Spitalfields Market)

'I'm finding that the younger generation are really into vinyl'

ALAN, DALLYSOUNDS

AQUAMARINE

14 Pierrepoint Row, Camden Passage,
Islington N1 8EF
0207 359 0197
www.aquamarineantiques.co.uk
Wed and Sat 9:00-17:30;
Mon, Tue, Thu, Fri and Sun 12:00-17:30
Angel Tube

A small shop amongst the secondhand gaggle of Pierrepoint Row, Aquamarine sells a strange but fascinating mix of militaria and taxidermy. Few are the shops in which stuffed lizards share shelf space with Nazi helmets. All of the military memorabilia, from fur lined flight jackets to Russian Imperial Flying Corp pilots' badges, is genuine.

BLACK GULL BOOKS

70 West Yard, Camden Lock,
Camden NW1 8AF
0207 267 5005
Mon-Sun 10:00-18:00
Camden Town Tube

Camden Lock's long-standing secondhand bookshop is a smart, well-ordered affair. The books are in good condition, some apparently unthumbed; indeed, you can find thrillers or literary fiction not long since off the printing press. They sell all sorts – from Jodi Picoult novels to biographies of Rasputin – although, as you might expect in this part of town, some of the categories have certain bohemian leanings, notably, the sizeable section of shelving apportioned to 'Sex, Drugs and Rock 'n' Roll'. The arts and philosophy are also well covered.

CHURCH STREET BOOKSHOP

142 Stoke Newington Church Street,
Stoke Newington N16 0JU
0207 241 5411
Mon-Sun 11:00-18:00
Stoke Newington Rail

A popular, unpretentious character on
Stoke Newington's vibrant main road,
Church Street bookshop has a wide-
ranging stock despite its relatively modest
proportions. All the mainstream genres
are featured, with travellers and children
particularly well catered for.

DODO

First Floor, Alfies Antique Market,
13-25 Church Street, Marylebone NW8 8DT
0207 706 1545
www.dodoposters.com
Tue-Sat 10:30-17:30
Marylebone/Edgware Road Tube

Dodo sells fantastic old advertising
posters dating as far back as the 1920s.
Some are huge, such as a three metre
high celebration of gravy that reads 'Ah
Bisto'. 'Guinness for Strength', 'Apples for
Health', 'Nivea Creme or Oil for Suntan
Skin Health and Beauty' – the guidance
is broad, kind of charming and lavishly
illustrated. Some of the best designs are
on travel posters, directing tourists to
Rhodesia, Davos and even Chessington
Zoo. The proprietor, Liz, is an expert on
all of it.

ELDICA

8 Bradbury Street, Dalston N16 8JN
0207 254 5220
www.eldica.co.uk
Tue-Sat 11:30-19:00; Sun 12:00-19:00
Dalston Kingsland Tube

Eldica began life as a Spitalfields stall,
and today, removed to a permanent
home just off Kingsland High Street in
Dalston, it retains a casual, friendly and
pleasingly cluttered air. The back half
of the small shop is devoted to old vinyl
with a preference for soul, funk, jazz, rap
and reggae. A turntable lets you listen
before you buy. The front half of the
shop is stuffed with secondhand clothes,
homeware, magazines, curtains, books
and bits of furniture, much of it treading
the perilous 1970s path between kitsch
and criminal.

FLASHBACK

50 Essex Road, Islington N1 8LR
0207 354 9356
www.flashback.co.uk
Mon-Sat 10:00-19:00; Sun 12:00-18:00
Angel/Highbury and Islington Tube

A much-loved crate-digger's paradise with
a smaller sibling in Crouch End (at 144
Crouch Hill), Flashback prides itself on
an egalitarian approach to secondhand
music. The range is broad – from Muddy
Waters to Joy Division – the prices are fair
and the quality good. Vinyl (including a
good selection of genuine rarities), CDs
and DVDs are all sold.

£££-£££

HAGGLE VINYL

114 Essex Road, Islington N1 8LX
0207 704 3101
www.hagglevinyl.com
Mon-Sun 10:00-18:00
Angel Tube

Haggle Vinyl, as owner Lynn Alexander points out, is more than a shop. It's an experience. Located on the busy road leading out of Islington's gentrified heart towards Dalston, the place is stuffed with old records (there are no CDs here) – all of it bought from the public. Walls, ceiling, floor and brimming racks spill with vinyl of every genre and age. Piles of old 45s tower precariously, daring the visitor to attempt any kind of rummage. Browse for long enough and no doubt you'll find a collectible gem, although Lynn suggests he's more concerned with selling music that will make you smile, than completing your collection of rare, mono pressings. Lynn is something of a legend in these parts: a characterful, wryly comedic expert or something of an obdurate curmudgeon, depending on your outlook. Take your thickest skin, try to go with the flow when the opinions start rolling – and you should enjoy the experience.

£££

LUCKY SEVEN (AND LUCKY PAD)

127 Stoke Newington Church Street,
Stoke Newington N16 0UH
07990 558062
Mon-Sun 11:00-19:00
Stoke Newington Rail

A secondhand record shop that also sells used books, Lucky Seven is the kind of snug, friendly and informal place that makes browsing for old stuff a total joy. The front room is mostly vinyl filled, with the full spectrum covered, from Northern Soul to Techno. A couple of shelves house books, DVDs and old comics of the Marvel and DC variety. A backroom is filled with cheaper stuff – vinyl, magazines, books and videos – all of it haphazardly arranged and priced somewhere around the 50p mark. Down some Dickensian stairs, past ancient flock wallpaper and bare brickwork, another small room is packed with men's, women's and children's vintage clothes and homeware, trading under the moniker Lucky Pad. Throw in a few kitsch 50s painting and you've got a secondhand blowout that does Stoke Newington proud.

🅒🅐🅔-🅒🅐🅔

PSYCHOTRONIC

**30D Second Floor Market Hall,
Camden Lock NW1 8AL
07719 512461
Wed, Thu, Sat, Sun 13:00-18:00
Camden Town Tube**

You have to work a bit to find Psychotronic – negotiating the stairs to the upper, indoor reaches of Camden Lock market – but it's worth the effort. The contents reside at the more offbeat end of 20th century popular culture. It's a mix of cult film (horror, biker, exploitation, etc.) memorabilia, from *Creature from the Black Lagoon* toys to *Alien* props, and magazines, pin up posters, toys, games and other random collectibles dating back as far as the 1930s. If you're in the market for a gyrating go-go dancer drink-mixer from the 1960s, this is where to come.

© £ £ - © £ £

RESURRECTION RECORDS

228 Camden High Street, Camden NW1 8QS
01823 413846
www.resurrectionmusic.com
Mon-Sun 10:30-17:45
Camden Town Tube

Resurrection Records, squirreled away in the artificial light of a Camden basement, has all the visual charm of a cardboard box. But then who needs fancy décor when you're shopping for secondhand industrial, gothic, punk and metal vinyl? From the Pixies, to the Fields of the Nephilim and the Revolting Cocks, the selection is good and cheap.

© £ £

VINCENT FREEMAN

1 Camden Passage, Islington N1 8EA
0207 226 6178
www.vincentfreemanantiques.com
Wed/Sat 10:30-16:30; or by appointment
Angel Tube

A small, intriguing Camden Passage shop selling antique music boxes, singing birds (the coin operated, gilded cage variety) and automata. Most of the ornate cylindrical and disc music boxes date from the later 19th century, made by the likes of Bremond, Paillard, Regina and Nicole Freres.

WALDEN BOOKS

38 Harmood Street, Camden NW1 8DP
0207 267 8146
www.waldenbooks.co.uk
Thu-Sun 10:30-18:30
Chalk Farm/Camden Town Tube

The tumult of Chalk Farm Road recedes
rapidly as you stroll along Harmood
Street and discover Walden Books,
a long-time occupant on this largely
residential road. The bookcases in front
of the shop hold cheap popular literature,
from JRR Tolkien to John Updike. Inside,
the honey coloured shelves harbour
more academically orientated books,
on art, literature, philosophy, poetry,
natural history or theatre, many of them
out of print. It's the place to come for a
biography of Wagner or an old copy of
Rabelais' *Gargantua*. The shop also has
a particularly good selection of books
on London.

⚅££

BOOKMONGERS

439 Coldharbour Lane, Brixton SW9 8LN
0207 738 4225
Mon-Sat 10:30-18:30
Brixton Tube

Bookmongers has got something
traders must search long and hard for.
Atmosphere. You can't see the walls for
books; there's a sofa and a sleeping dog;
a Wynton Marsalis record plays in the
background. It's somewhere to linger, to
browse. And the choice is vast. It begins
with a great shelf of comedy books by
the door, moves through a monumental
fiction section (arranged, unusually,
by author gender), on past cookery,
fantasy, literature, music, cinema, theatre,
graphic novels, health and foreign
language sections, and ends with the
aforementioned sofa, some old copies
of *National Geographic* and a collection
of bargain books selling at 50p each.
Make sure you've cleared an hour in your
schedule before setting foot inside.

MY BACK PAGES

🅑£££-£££

8-10 Balham Station Road, Balham SW12 9SG
0208 675 9346
Mon-Sat 10:00-19:00; Sun 11:00-18:00
Balham Tube

First things first: the name. As Doug, jocular owner of Balham's stalwart secondhand bookshop explains, *My Back Pages* appropriates the name of a Bob Dylan song. The shop's continued survival may be down to the breadth of the stock. Books on hill walking, black writing and American literature sit amongst more typical sections of fiction (a vast collection), thrillers, travel guides, children's books, poetry and so on. There's a particularly good selection of history books, and even a good range of new fiction titles. "I've always sold books of every description in my shop, and I've always tried to be democratic about who those books will appeal to," says Doug. "Even today, when there are so many options for buying a book, I think people still enjoying having a browse in a bookshop. Perhaps it offers a rare chance to reject the headlong race to modernity." You can see his point. Half an hour lost in the shelves of My Back Pages is time well spent.

'I've always sold books of every description in my shop, and I've always tried to be democratic about who those books will appeal to'

DOUG, MY BACK PAGES

££-£££

143-145 Lee High Road, Lewisham SE13 5PF
0208 244 3771
www.accordions.co.uk
Mon 14:00-18:00; Tue,
Thu and Fri 10:30-18:00; Sat 10:30-17:00
Lewisham DLR/Hither Green Rail

The spirit of Lewisham's remarkable squeezebox shop (the biggest in the UK) is summed up in one instrument. Dating back to 1930s, it sits on the busy shelves, adorned with little more decoration than the name of its maker, Bruno Allodi. Today, Bruno's son, Emilio, upholds the family tradition, selling and repairing secondhand (and new) accordions. Some date back to the 1920s; most have been made since the 1960s. In common, all have been overhauled by Emilio. "The accordion has become far more popular over the last ten to 15 years," he explains. "It's used a lot more on recordings now, and more children are taking the instrument up – we recently completed an order of accordions for schools in the local authority."

'The accordion has become far more popular over the last ten to 15 years

EMILIO, ALLODI ACCORDIONS

ALLODI ACCORDIONS

(At the Beehive), 330-332 Creek Road, Greenwich SE10 9SW
0208 858 1964
Mon-Sun 10:30-18:00
Cutty Sark DLR

Brothers Tony and Graham ran a record stall on Greenwich Market for 25 years before they opened a permanent shop nearby two years ago (within The Beehive, sharing space with UMI and Co vintage clothing (see chapter one). They look at home in the new setting, surrounded by a mix of secondhand and new vinyl. All genres are covered, although the brothers confess a weakness for 1960s and 70s bands. Rarities (mono top loading *White Album* anyone?) rub shoulders with run-of-the-mills, overlooked by old copies of *Melody Maker*, vintage soft porn magazines and a mildly unsettling leopard skin carpet on the ceiling. The Casbah rocks, as Joe Strummer nearly said.

Casbah Records

GRAMEX

25 Lower Marsh, Waterloo SE1 7RJ
0207 401 3830
Mon-Sat 11:00-19:00
Waterloo/Lambeth North Tube

"Would you like a tea or a coffee?"
Not a typical opener in the traditional
shopkeeper/customer dialogue. But
Roger, the ever-present owner of
Gramex, isn't typical. Neither is his
shop. It sells secondhand CDs, records,
78s and cylinders (the pre-cursor to the
record), the majority of them classical.
A selection of jazz records has been
added to the basement in recent years,
apparently by popular demand. The
original Gramophone Record Exchange
(aka Gramex) opened in Angel over a
century go, the pride of George Russell,
retired Boer War officer. Roger first met
George in 1949, and 30 years ago took
over the store himself, by then relocated
to Waterloo. Two million record sales
later, he wants you to sit in a comfy chair,
to have a coffee, to peruse the extensive
stock and, if you want, to listen before
buying. Roger has an encyclopaedic
knowledge of music, opera in particular,
and will talk you through any of the
CDs stacked, unordered, on the 'latest
arrivals' table in the middle of the shop.
Chat for long enough and he'll offer you a
sandwich to go with your coffee. Brilliant.

CURIOSITY
Celebrity
DOLLS

HALCYON BOOKS

**1 Greenwich South Street,
Greenwich SE10 8NW
0208 305 2675
www.halcyonbooks.co.uk
Mon-Sat 10:00-18:00
Greenwich/Cutty Sark DLR**

A five-minute stroll from the busy heart of Greenwich, Halcyon Books is a small but pleasingly well-stocked shop. There's no particular area of speciality amid the secondhand books, but all persuasions are well catered for, with a vertiginous wall of paperback fiction (there's a ladder, should you need one), shelves of history, poetry and cookery books, and a low-level bookcase packed with children's stories. Prints, maps and vintage magazines can also be had. And the prices are good too.

NAVAL AND MARITIME BOOKS

**66 Royal Hill, Greenwich SE10 8RT
0208 692 1794
www.navalandmaritimebooks.com
Wed-Sat 10:00-18:00
Greenwich/Cutty Sark DLR**

Anthony and Setitia have been selling naval, maritime, travel and exploration books in Greenwich for almost 30 years. As Anthony explains, they're well placed: "Visitors to the National Maritime Museum, just up the road, get excited by something they see there, on Nelson for example, and then find our shop and realise they can read up on the subject." Some of the books, in what is a charming shop, date back to the 18th century. From a contemporary account of the 1750 execution of Admiral Byng to a 1935 guide to the *Port of London*, the shop covers its chosen subjects from every conceivable angle.

🄰🄱£-🄰🄱🄲

ROBERT MORLEY AND COMPANY (PIANOS)

34 Engate Street, Lewisham SE13 7HA
0208 318 5838
www.morleypianos.co.uk
Mon-Sat 9:30-17:00
Lewisham DLR/Ladywell Rail

The Morley family has been selling pianos in Lewisham for 130 years. Today, the company makes harpsichords and clavichords (the compact, softly spoken forebear of the piano), alongside selling and restoring secondhand and antique pianos and harps. The prices vary significantly with age and model, from a 1950s Marshall and Rose upright, through the early 20th century Bechstein grands and on to the likes of a 1780 Christopher Garner square piano, an instrument contemporaneous with Mozart. The business takes a conservative approach to restoration: "We tend to think they should sound as they were meant to sound. Not like a new Yamaha," confirms Julia Morley, sixth generation piano seller.

SECONDHAND BOOKS

20 Lower Marsh, Waterloo SE1 7RJ
Wed-Fri 11:00-19:00
Waterloo/Lambeth North Tube

Simply named and simply stocked, Secondhand Books is a pleasing Waterloo antidote to the high street giants of the modern book trade. The books here are drawn from across the genres, although there's a preponderance of biographies. You won't find rows of Grisham or Cornwell, but you will find unexpected gems, such as a 1927 edition of Henrich Heine's *Italian Travel Sketches*.

SOUTHBANK BOOK MARKET

Under the arches of Waterloo Bridge
Mon-Sun late morning-early evening
Waterloo Tube

A pitch on the Southbank river walkway makes this small market the busiest (and most scenic) secondhand bookseller in London. The choice isn't bad, although it's inevitably limited to whatever the traders can fit on two or three long tables under the shelter of the bridge. Paperback novels, cookbooks and poetry anthologies rub shoulders with a few rarer books, not least a collection of mid 20th century Pelican titles (an old Penguin imprint). The market also sells repro lithographic prints and maps.

HOME & GARDEN

Furniture / Lighting
Bicycles / Electronics
Homewares / Salvage

A TRAWL AROUND LONDON'S SECONDHAND FURNITURE, LIGHTING AND ELECTRICAL SHOPS WILL TURN UP EVERYTHING YOU NEED TO FURNISH YOUR OWN HOME. FROM SLEEK MID-CENTURY MODERN TO BRASH 1970S COLOUR, THERE'S SOMETHING FOR ALL TASTES AND BUDGETS.

Amongst these shops a few genuine London junkyards survive. See them whilst you can, for their days may be numbered. In amongst the pub furniture and stuffed birds there will be things that will look good in your home (irrespective of price or pedigree), as well as no small amount of kitsch. More often the traditional junk shop has evolved into something more upmarket, where 20th century furniture and homeware, often carefully restored and announced as shabby chic or even 'upcycled', are sold as design pieces. They're inspiring shops, reusing and reimagining objects that would have been discarded a few years back.

Northwest London, along the Portobello and Golborne roads, is particularly good for furniture, whilst the permanent indoor markets like Alfies in Marylebone can eat up a whole day of your time with their secondhand lighting, furniture and homeware traders. The shops selling used hi-fi, televisions and computers are less common, but the ones that have survived the Internet age have done so by their expertise and reliability, and are duly well worth a visit.

At London's reclamation yards you find larger secondhand objects for the home. Even if you're not buying, the yards are worth a browse. Each gives an evocative insight into the London of old – a world of gas lamps, Crapper toilets and opulent chandeliers.

LAST PLACE ON EARTH

305-307 Portobello Road,
Notting Hill W10 5TD
0208 962 8741
Mon-Sun 11:00-17:00
Ladbroke Grove Tube

There's a bit of everything, not least a very pleasant coffee shop, in the two premises, located side by side, that comprise Last Place on Earth. Vintage clothes, lighting and books are all in evidence, although secondhand furniture makes up the majority of the stock. Most of it is unremarkable and relatively cheap, from 1970s dining chairs to pine corner cupboards, but a handful of older pieces – Art Deco drinks cabinets and the like – are worth the visit.

The Royal Borough of Kensington and Chelsea
PORTOBELLO ROAD, W.11

TALES FROM THE FARM

As you wander in and out of the furniture shops and antique arcades of the Portobello and Golborne roads, be aware that 150 years ago you would have been dodging cowpats. Only in the mid 19th century did Portobello Farm, the land surrounding the old country road, succumb to urbanisation. The arrival of the Hammersmith and City Railway in 1864 – and Ladbroke Grove Station with it – sealed its fate. Elegant terraces and town houses soon followed, establishing the area's well-heeled reputation. As for the name, Portobello Road took inspiration from Admiral Edward Vernon's victory at Puerto Bello, Panama, in 1739.

THE OLD CINEMA

160 Chiswick High Road, Chiswick W4 1PR
0208 995 4166
www.theoldcinema.co.uk
Mon-Sat 10:00-18:00; Sun 12:00-17:00
Turnham Green Tube

Chiswick's converted Edwardian picturehouse is rightly fabled for its salvaged vintage. The savvy owners have stocked it with furniture from all decades of the 20th century, bar, perhaps, the last couple. Sleek Scandinavian chairs from the 1950s are sold alongside Art Deco dressing tables and pre-war club chairs. The range is impressive, the prices strong but palatable. The Old Cinema also sells some great 'upcycled' objects, such as the blue elephant sculpted from old fruit cans and wooden tennis rackets turned into mirrors. All this and loads of vintage lighting too, from industrial to studio.

OLLIE & BOW

69 Golborne Road, Notting Hill W10 5NP
07768 790725
Tue-Sat 10:00-17:00 (closed Thu)
Westbourne Park/Ladbroke Grove Tube

Not many secondhand furniture shops make you laugh. Ollie & Bow, an ostensibly scruffy shop situated just off Portobello Road's less genteel end, however, is a definite mood lifter. From the seven-foot tall gorilla model (its origins unclear) to the kitsch stony-faced ceramic lion, old leather boxing gloves strung over its ear, the stock is original, eccentric and amusing. Piled up amid the oddities some fine old lighting and furniture, such as a high-backed patina-rich leather Victorian Chesterfield, set Ollie & Bow apart.

POP BOUTIQUE

6 Monmouth Street,
Covent Garden WC2H 9HB
0207 497 5262
www.pop-boutique.com
Mon-Sat 11:00-19:00; Sun 13:00-18:00
Covent Garden/Tottenham Court Road Tube

London's outpost of the Pop Boutique chain sells a good mix of cheap pre-loved clothes, recycled garments (new shirts made from vintage fabric) and jewellery (not least a good crop of authentic 1960s cufflinks), but is perhaps of more interest for its secondhand homeware. It falls into the 'props from Abigail's Party' bracket: dial-up phones from the 60s and 70s, Scandinavian glassware, vinyl records and outrageously patterned lampshades. Is that Demis Roussos I can hear on the stereo?

X ELECTRICAL

125 King Street, Hammersmith W6 9JG
0208 563 7383
www.xelectrical.com
Mon-Sat 10:00-18:00
Hammersmith/Ravenscourt Park Tube

The majority of X Electrical's Hammersmith store is filled with secondhand audio and visual electronic equipment. It's a mix of musical equipment (hi-fi systems and separates), musical instruments (of the plug 'em in variety) and DJ equipment, computers, home cinema, camcorders, TVs and games consoles. The staff know their stuff and everything is tested before being sold with a warranty. They also seem to cater to all budgets

€€€-€€€

BACON STREET SALVAGE

12 Bacon Street, Shoreditch E1 6LF
0207 613 4672
Mon-Sun 9:00-17:00
Shoreditch High Street Rail
Aldgate East Tube

The end lock-up on Bacon Street is stuffed with old catering equipment and the assorted utensils of commercial life. Fridges and large stainless steel sinks spill out onto the street, whilst woks, well-used pans, display cabinets, indestructible old safes and boxes of assorted casters characterise the stock inside. Much of the stuff here is sold on to businesses, but have a root around and you'll find something for the home, not least industrial lighting that falls just on the required shabby side of chic.

€€€-€€€

C.E. BURNS & SONS
(AKA THE PERSIAN MARKET)

16-22 Bacon Street, Shoreditch E1 6LF
0207 739 6270
Mon-Fri 9:00-16:00; Sat 9:00-13:00
Shoreditch High Street Rail/
Aldgate East Tube

This secondhand office furniture warehouse, also known as the Persian Market, is woven into the fabric of the East End. The owners, the Burns family, have been trading around Brick Lane for decades. Charlie Burns (known to most as Uncle Charlie), in his 90s, is the paterfamilias. He's the original 'recycler', a former paper merchant of such renown that he was made a Freeman of the City of London; a man granted an audience with Pope John Paul II no less. Today, he can usually be found sitting in his car in front of the shop. The shop itself, a dark, deep lock-up, is full of good and cheap desks, tables, fans, filing cabinets, chairs and the like.

£££

ELEMENTAL

67 Brushfield Street, Spitalfields E1 6AA
0207 247 7588
www.elemental.uk.com
Tue-Sun 11:00-18:00
Liverpool Street Tube

Elemental restores and 'upcycles' old utilitarian furniture and lighting, creating high design for the domestic environment. Old filing cabinets are pared back to brushed steel, 1950s factory lamps are reconditioned and old water tanks reimagined as coffee tables. Dentist's chairs, coat hooks, factory clocks and school benches: in the right house this stuff can look incredible.

LE GRENIER

ⓔⓔ£-ⓔⓔⓔ

146 Bethnal Green Road, Shoreditch E2 6DG
0207 790 7379
www.le-grenier.com
Mon-Sat 12:00-19:00 (closed Wed);
Sun 10:00-19:00
Shoreditch High Street Overground/
Aldgate East Tube

Yuko and Jean-Louis opened Le Grenier three years ago. In the midst of London's thrifty-chic Shoreditch heartland, they've worked hard to distinguish the shop from its near competitors, a feat achieved by positioning homeware, furniture (not so old but very *de jour*) and assorted curiosities, alongside the ubiquitous rack of vintage clothes. "We wanted to make Le Grenier something a bit different," confirms Yuko, a calming, affable presence in what is a fairly thronged shop on a busy road. A Second World War German Wehrmacht pony fur backpack, apparently used by medical troops in an alpine division, seems likely to be the only one on sale in London. Ditto the First World War French pilot's riding boots, complete with wooden soles; and perhaps even the classic Vitra office chair. Old tobacco tins, jewellery and Hornsea pottery are amongst the less exotic items. "Quite a lot of what we sell is sourced in France," Yuko explains. "We choose things for the shop that we like personally. Which is why our house looks like a stock room! Some of it can't be used in its current form, and so we adapt it, such as the bits of 1950s wallpaper that we've turned into greetings cards."

€££

SECONDHAND LOCK-UP

Railways Arches, Brick Lane, Shoreditch
07951 964963
Mon-Sun 8:00-18:00
Shoreditch High Street Rail/
Liverpool Street Tube

Brick Lane is bisected by the new East London rail line. Where it crosses the road, bits of the old Victorian bridge have been left standing aside the new concrete structure. Under this crumbling brickwork, on the northern side of the line amid the remnants of a Georgian stable, a lock-up with large red wooden doors is packed to the rafters with secondhand stuff. A lot of it's practical – pots and pans, microwaves, bikes, even a couple of old Durst black and white photographic enlargers accompanied by a mobile dark room – but there's also plenty for the mantelpiece, from china dogs to paintings and old radios. The snack bar inside means you can browse around with tea and bagel in hand.

THE SECOND HAND STORE

£££-£££

14 Bacon Street, Shoreditch E1 6LF
07973 324814
Mon-Sun 11:00-17:00
Shoreditch High Street Rail/
Liverpool Street Tube

Take a deep breath before you cross the innocuous, unmarked threshold to the Second Hand Store (it's one away from the end of Bacon Street, off Brick Lane). You could be in there for quite some time. Furniture, picture frames, ladders, flags, lights, cutlery, old 45s, tools, toys, chandeliers, books, televisions, glassware – short of animals and vegetables, they seem to have it covered. Apparently, it's a favourite haunt for filmmakers in search of props. The arrangement of items is fairly chaotic, so you'll need to root around, something that the friendly owner, Des, is happy to abide. If you find something you like, ask him for a price.

STRATFORD COMPUTER FAIR

£££

98 Gibbins Road, Stratford E15 2HU
Sat-Sun 10:30-16:00
Stratford Tube/Stratford DLR

Held in a sports hall close to Stratford Station (you can see it from the DLR platform), this weekender is a rare survivor of the computer fair world, persevering where most have given up in the face of online competition. The best thing about it is the chance to pick up and examine what you buy, whether it's a used hard drive, printer, keyboard, video card or laptop.

THE TEA ROOMS

**The Old Truman Brewery, next to
146 Brick Lane, Shoreditch E1 6QL
Sat 11:00-18:00; Sun 10:00-17:00
Shoreditch High Street Rail/
Liverpool Street Tube**

Under the Old Vat House of the Truman
Brewery, the Tea Rooms is a fixed indoor
weekend market of around 15 traders.
Most sell once functional but now largely
ornamental items: typewriters, old leather
luggage cases, gramophones and the
like. It's a good place for kitsch – for a
framed flamenco dancer print that had
its heyday in a Blackpool B&B circa 1977,
or a chipped plaster-of-Paris Jesus. The
Tea Rooms also features a couple of
jewellery and clothes stalls, alongside
a pleasant café.

VINTAGE HEAVEN

££-£££ (icons)

82 Columbia Road, Bethnal Green E2 7QB
01277 215968
www.vintageheaven.co.uk
Fri by appointment; Sat 12:00-18:00;
Sun 8:30-17:00
Bethnal Green Tube

"When I had to start hiring garages to store it all in I knew I had a problem." Margaret, the effervescent owner of Vintage Heaven, is explaining why she opened a shop. Almost everything on sale here comes from her own personal collection of china and glass. Most of it dates somewhere between the 1930s and the 70s, but some of the china is older, from as far back as Edwardian and even late Victorian days. "I want people to buy it to use," says Margaret. "There's something so emotional about buying secondhand; people come in, see a certain cup or a plate, and immediately they're taken back to childhood, to their grandmother's kitchen or somewhere similar." Vintage Heaven sells complete sets of china, but also has odds and sods, notably on the table set aside for orphaned cups and saucers, alongside a few bits of furniture, framed pictures, linen and books, all of it at good prices. There's even a café, Cake Hole, at the back of the shop.

WESTLAND

£££ (icons)

St Michael's Church, Leonard Street,
Shoreditch EC2A 4ER
0207 739 8094
www.westlandlondon.com
Mon-Fri 9:00-18:00; Sat 10:00-17:00
Old Street/Liverpool Street Tube

Westland's home inside a Grade I listed James Brookes church is well suited for showing off the grand fireplaces, chandeliers and wooden panelling salvaged from what must have been equally grand properties around Europe. Gothic Revival pedestals, Corinthian columns carved in wood, 19th century coaching lamps and even 19th century church bells – Westland is a paean to the decorative interiors of yore.

THE ARCHITECTURAL FORUM/N1 ARCHITECTURAL SALVAGE

312-314 Essex Road, Islington N1 3AX
0207 704 0982
www.thearchitecturalforum.com
Mon-Sat 10:00-17:00
Highbury & Islington Tube

One business, two locations on the same small Islington block, kept apart by a no-frills caff. The Architectural Forum is the slick, elegant showroom side, filled with fine fireplaces, chandeliers, restored industrial lights and other items reclaimed and made shiny. Two doors down, the N1 Architectural Salvage yard has the things that are safe to leave out in the rain – cast iron radiators awaiting attention, roll top baths, chimney pots and flagstones.

ATOMIUM

Unit D18, Horse Tunnel Market, Chalk Farm Road, Camden NW1 8AH
0207 485 8634
www.atomium.co.uk
Thu 12:00-17:00; Fri-Sun 10:30-18:00
Camden Town/Chalk Farm Tube

Naughty magazines from the 60s look remarkably tame now, the prevalence of wicker furniture possibly more shocking than the nudity. Indeed, today they're over-the-counter collectors' items. Find them in the impressively diverse Atomium, stockists of well chosen mid 20th century design-led secondhand stuff, selling everything from modernist furniture, 1960s Swedish glassware and a Dansette record player to old dress patterns, books and the aforementioned magazines.

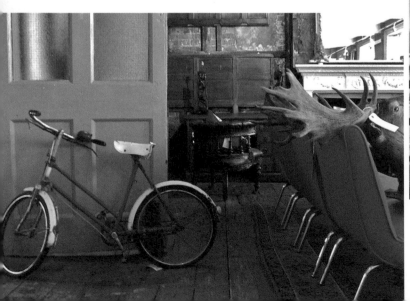

AUDIO GOLD

308-310 Park Road, Crouch End N8 8LA
0208 341 9007
www.audiogold.co.uk
Mon-Sat 10:30-18:30
Highgate Tube

There aren't many bricks and mortar shops left selling secondhand hi-fi in the Internet age, so Audio Gold is something of a rare treat (although they do sell online). Most of the audio equipment dates to the 1980s and 90s – apparently halcyon days for the hi-fi – although some items, such as the wind-up gramophones, are considerably older. The staff can build a system to match your requirements, including hooking the pre-loved stuff up to your MP3 player, television and so on.

BETH

Ground Floor, Alfies Antique Market,
13-25 Church Street, Marylebone NW8 8DT
07776 136003
Tue-Sat 10:00-17:00
Marylebone/Edgware Road Tube

Beth, the vivacious proprietor of her eponymous shop, has a passion for Art Deco. "I like it because the geometric shapes broke away from the stiff and often dour style of the Edwardians," she says. Not that her shop full of collectibles is limited to the Art Deco period. The shelves feature ceramics by Clarice Cliff, Shelley, Paragon and Ainsley, Czech glass from the 1970s, ceiling lamps from the 40s and much more.

®££-®£®

CAMDEN CYCLES

251 Eversholt Street, Camden NW1 1BA
020 7388 7899
www.camdencycles.co.uk
Mon-Fri 9:00-19:00; Sat 9:00-18:00;
Sun 11:00-17:00
Mornington Crescent Tube

It's a mystery why there aren't more
secondhand cycle shops in London, given
the number of two wheeled commuters
around and the problems inherent in
buying a shiny new bike (like catnip to
any self-respecting thief). Camden Cycles
is one of the few, and it does a fantastic
job. Some of the bikes sold here are what
the proprietor, Ali, describes as 'vintage'
but the majority are only a few years old.
Most are sourced from Police and Council
auctions. Each leaves the shop with a
month's free service, and customers are
welcome to pitch Ali for a part exchange
deal on their existing bike. The only flaw –
they don't sell children's bikes.

THE COBBLED YARD

1 Bouverie Road, Stoke Newington N16 0AH
0208 809 5286
www.cobbled-yard.co.uk
Tue-Sun 11:00-18:00
Stoke Newington Rail

An oasis of calm in a former Hansom cab
stable block off busy Stoke Newington
Church Street, The Cobbled Yard sells
secondhand furniture. Some items
are antique, but most date from the
Edwardian period through to the later 20th
century. Chesterfields, farmhouse tables
and mirrors, all in reasonable condition if
not mint, are typical items. One old stable
space within the yard is crammed with
dining room chairs.

Curiosity

'People relate to objects like they relate to songs; they evoke such strong memories'

BEVERLEY, CURIOSITY

Unit 90C, Stables Market, Camden NW1 8AH
07850 478884
Mon-Fri 11:00-19:00; Sat-Sun 10:00-19:00
Camden Town/Chalk Farm Tube

"People relate to objects like they relate to songs; they evoke such strong memories." Beverley is explaining the ethos behind Curiosity, a Camden Stables shop of collectibles and ephemera. Ceramics, including teapots for every occasion, loom large in the philosophy, but there are also great collections of cameras, dolls and old prints. She creates installations around the shop, gathering objects thematically. So, there's the Ice Lake, with ceramic swans on a glass tray, and The Pub, featuring tankards and the like. It's borderline nuts, but brilliant nonetheless.

⚉⚉⚉
DECORATUM

In the basement of Alfies Antique Market,
13-25 Church Street, Marylebone NW8 8DT
0207 724 6969
www.decoratum.com
Tue-Sat 10:00-18:00
Marylebone/Edgware Road Tube

Decoratum and its mid to late 20th century furniture occupies the entire basement of Alfies Antique Market. It's top end stuff. Worthy of a design museum no less. Chairs by Jacques Henri Varichon, Charles Eames and Percival Lafer are typical. The tables, mirrors and lighting, from Venini 'spun sugar' chandeliers to Mole Richardson Chrome studio spots, are equally pedigreed. As are the prices, naturally. Artwork by Peter Blake and Antonio de Felipe watches over the furniture.

££££-£££

MR ALL SORTS

191 Northchurch Road, Islington N1 3NT
0207 359 1791
Mon-Sat 9:00-18:00
Highbury & Islington Tube

This earthy, dark and wholly excellent
den of a shop represents something of a
dying breed within London's secondhand
landscape. It isn't polished, ordered or
appropriately lit (unless you prefer to
view objects in near darkness before
you buy) but it is a genuine original. Mr
All Sorts has been spilling its contents
of old furniture, fireplaces, mirrors
and chandeliers out onto the Islington
pavement for over three decades.
Furniture is the mainstay, both outside
and in; most of it post 1900 and most of it
in good condition, but you may well also
find giant shop sign letters, canon balls
and books.

££££-£££

ODYSSEY

11 Pierrepoint Arcade, Camden Passage,
Islington N1 8EF
07970 635158
Wed 9:00-15:30; Thu-Fri 13:00-18:00;
Sat 9:00-17:00; Sun 13:00-18:00
Angel Tube

Standing out from the somewhat
musty bric-a-brac crowd of Islington's
Pierrepoint Arcade, Odyssey is a gem
of a place specialising in lighting and
glassware from the second half of the
20th century. The owner, Paul, knows his
stuff. He's particularly keen on Italian
lighting and Swedish and Czech coloured
glass. The ceiling is straight out of
Barbarella; witness the bulbous rise and
fall light resembling a beige jellyfish. On
the shelves, Alsterfors glass and bits of
Poole Delphis Pottery are colourful and
highly collectible. The shop also sells
post-war furniture, a lot of it Formica clad.
Encouragingly, Paul is determined his
prices will continue to compete with what
you'll find on the Internet.

💷💷💷-💷💷💷

PELICANS AND PARROTS

40 Stoke Newington Road, Dalston N16 7XJ
0203 215 2083
www.pelicansandparrots.com
Mon-Fri 12:00-20:00; Sat 11:00-20:00;
Sun 12:00-19:00
Dalston Kingsland Tube

Imagine if Sherlock Holmes was alive today and living in Dalston. Surely he'd shop at Pelicans and Parrots. The disparate objects on sale, from a stuffed bird in a glass case to a 1960s turntable unit, are somehow made congruent in combination. The shop's whitewashed walls and generally sunny demeanour certainly helps. As co-owner Chuko explains, Pelicans and Parrots is more about trend-based vintage than any specific era. And so women's and men's labelled fashion from mid 20th century onwards mingles harmoniously with new furniture, an Arco style light, framed photos, old copies of the *Face* and the antlered hunting trophies on the walls. In short, a fascinating shop.

💷💷💷

OOH-LA-LA!

147 Holloway Road, Holloway N7 8LX
0207 609 0455
Mon 11:00-18:00; Tue-Sat 10:00-18:00
Holloway Road/Highbury and Islington Tube

Ooh-La-La! sells secondhand furniture, clothes and collectibles for the home. From the weird and wonderful to the elegant and timeless, the stock roams across eras and styles. A fabulously bulbous 1960s TV sits atop a 17th century oak coffer, whilst an old theodolite stands tall amid typewriters, a guitar amp and a stuffed fox. Above it all, up on a shelf, a genuine 50s mannequin of James Dean, complete with cigarette, looks on nonplussed. In particular, Ooh-La-La! has a very good selection of vintage lamps and lights. It's a busy, interesting shop just on the right side of cluttered.

PRIMROSE HILL INTERIORS

£££

115 Regents Park Road,
Primrose Hill NW1 8UR
0207 722 6622
www.essentialvintage.com
Tue-Sat 11:00-18:00; Sun 12:00-17:00
Chalk Farm Tube

The furniture at Primrose Hill Interiors resides at the top end of vintage. Indeed, some of it, a sublime Maria Theresa Venetian Mirror for example, is antique, although the myriad styles of the 20th century, from Art Deco to Scandinavian modernist, comprise most of the elegant stock. Lighting, art, designer and dress jewellery, and objets d'art are also sold.

SARGENT AND CO

£££

74 Mountgrove Road, Finsbury Park N5 2LT
0207 359 7642
www.sargentandco.com
Wed-Sat 10:30-18:30
Arsenal/Finsbury Park Tube

A marvellous north London bike shop that seems to be enjoying life back in the 1970s, selling and repairing the kind of drop handle-barred machines that Eddie Merckx used to get about on. Competition bikes, touring bikes and tandems, some dating back as far as the 1930s, are sold alongside bespoke affairs made up to your particular requirements. They also do road bike repairs and restorations.

THE SECOND HAND YARD

€€€

Marton Road (the Church Street end),
Stoke Newington N16 0RA
07903 185813
Wed-Sun early until late
Stoke Newington Rail

Think about the Conran Shop. Now try picturing the polar opposite. Gathered haphazardly along and behind a wall in Stoke Newington, the used furniture traders here refer, rather loosely, to their patch as the Second Hand Yard. They're a friendly bunch, Irish John at their head, happy to let you browse through the paintings, clocks, wardrobes, tables and random items that comprise the stock. On some days a tarot card reader sets up in their midst. In particular, the yard brims with secondhand chairs. At first glance nothing here appears to carry much collectible value – although a sustained search could turn up who knows what – but it's a great place to find cheap, functional furniture. Take cash.

STEPHEN LAZARUS

€€€

First Floor, Alfies Antique Market,
13-25 Church Street, Marylebone NW8 8DT
07981 374909
Mon-Sat 10:00-17:00
Marylebone/Edgware Road Tube

Stephen deals in various decorative objects and pieces of furniture from the 20th century, but it's the lights in his Marylebone shop that make the greatest impact. They fill the shop, literally, an impenetrable forest of chrome, steel, enamel and glass. Some are old factory lights; others are desk lamps or film set lights – all are 20th century. In common, each has been gracefully restored. A few, like the bulbous street lamps mounted on old wooden tripods or the spindly-limbed industrial French wall lamps placed on a new base, have been adapted to suit a changed role. Ralph Lauren and Jamie Oliver are numbered amongst the clients.

VINCENZO CAFFARELLA

Ground Floor, Alfies Antique Market,
13-25 Church Street, Marylebone NW8 8DT
0207 724 3701
www.vinca.co.uk
Tue-Sat 10:00-18:00
Marylebone/Edgware Road Tube

Vincenzo and his partner, Monica, have two shops on Marylebone's Church St, the biggest on the ground floor of Alfies Antique Market. They specialise in Italian lighting, furniture and art from the 1950s to the 70s. The loud coloured discs of Murano chandeliers and bright patterns of a Fornasetti chair share space with the muted geometry of Stilnovo lights and Gio Ponti furniture. Pleasingly, the big names are mixed with more obscure designers, chosen for exuberance and originality. As Monica explains, Italian design from this period will work in any shape, size or age of home – it just needs some creative thinking.

£££

VINTAGE PLANET

**Unit D23 Horse Tunnel Market,
Chalk Farm Road, Camden NW1 8AH
Mon-Fri 12:00-18:30; Sat-Sun 10:30-19:00
Camden Town/Chalk Farm Tube**

The core of Vintage Planet's business is
secondhand clothes, but of perhaps more
interest is the shop's collection of 1970s
and 80s Polaroid cameras (for which you
can still buy the film) and ghetto blasters,
most of them in working order. They even
have two-track tape recorders that let you
party like its 1973.

SOUTHWEST

COLLECTIBLES

ⓔⓔⓔ

**82 Brixton Village, off Coldharbour Lane,
Brixton SW9 8PS
07507 669921
www.collectible-s.co.uk
Wed 11:00-15:00; Thu 10:00-22:00;
Fri 10:00-18:00; Sat 10:00-20:00;
Sun 11:00-16:30
Brixton Tube**

The old Granville Arcade (also known as Brixton Village) in Brixton is mid-gentrification, the old grocers, fishmongers and butchers now interspersed with modish cafés and shops like CollectibleS. Small boxy cameras, 1970s phones, old radios, prints in frames and bone china make up a good share of the stock. It's small, friendly and a perfect stop on any post-café meander.

LASSCO

ⓔⓔⓔ-ⓔⓔⓔ

**Brunswick House, 30 Wandsworth Road,
Vauxhall SW8 2LG
0207 394 2100
www.lassco.co.uk
Mon-Sat 10:00-17:00; Sun 11:00-17:00
Vauxhall Tube**

LASSCO is worth a visit for the premises alone, a hugely atmospheric Georgian townhouse. Apparently the gardens used to run down to the Thames; today tower blocks and roaring traffic hem the building in. The contents are fascinating. The architectural salvage includes floorboards, cast iron radiators, Edwardian toilets and the like, whilst the furniture ranges from Georgian dressers to rows of old cinema seats. Bakelite radios, dressmaker's dummies and rocking horses represent a small section of the other, myriad items within. You could spend hours here. Mercifully, it has an adjoining café-cum-restaurant.

NEW VINTAGE

**256 Battersea Park Road,
Battersea SW11 3BP
020 3490 6097
www.newvintage.co.uk
Mon-Wed 11:30-18:00; Thu 11:30-18:30;
Fri 12:00-18:00; Sat 10:30-18:00;
Sun 12:00-17:00
Clapham Junction Rail**

Julie Rumble's small Battersea shop sells vintage with a twist. The secondhand dressing tables, cupboards and chests of drawers here, all wooden and mostly mid 20th century, have been painted, papered or adorned with decoupage. She also sells a variety of old lampshades, tea sets and kitsch paintings, alongside bits of new furniture.

BLUE MANTLE

**The Old Fire Station, 306-312 Old Kent Road,
Bermondsey SE1 5UE
0207 703 7437
www.bluemantle.co.uk
Mon-Sat 10:30-17:30; Sun 14:30-18:30
(or by appt)
Elephant and Castle Tube**

You can't really miss London's biggest secondhand fireplace shop. It resides in a fantastic old fire station (it's blue 'Fire' lamp still attached) on the corner of the Old Kent and Shorncliffe Roads. Wooden, granite and marble surrounds, often stripped and restored, fill the building alongside cast iron grates, dog baskets and surround tiles. They also sell bits of furniture (both interior and garden), mirrors and chimney pots.

THE JUNK SHOP AND SPREAD EAGLE

💷💷💷–💷💷💷

9 Greenwich South Street,
Greenwich SE10 8NW
0208 305 1666
www.spreadeagle.org
Mon-Sun 10:00-18:00
Greenwich DLR

Like his father before him, Toby at the Spread Eagle presides over a marvellous pile of old junk. Today's place in Greenwich is the distillation of three older shops, their contents of books, antiques and curios brought together in one wholly pre-loved Georgian building. "I like the fact that we can sell anything," ponders Toby, leaning on a shelf stuffed with art books. Costume jewellery, Bakelite radios, dining chairs, lamps, taxidermy and stoneware hot water bottles crowd the shop's narrow walkways. Downstairs, ten additional traders sell everything from chandeliers to Neil Diamond records.

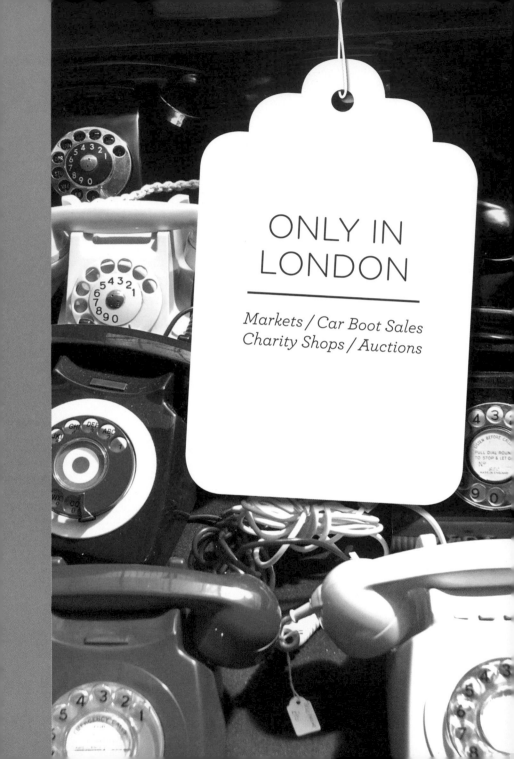

ONLY IN LONDON

Markets / Car Boot Sales
Charity Shops / Auctions

LONDON'S REAL CHARACTER IS LAID BARE IN THE CITY'S MARKETS, CAR BOOT SALES AND AUCTIONS. FROM GENTEEL CAMDEN PASSAGE TO NO-FRILLS NINE ELMS LANE, HERE YOU FIND THE MODERN, MULTICULTURAL CITY, BUT HERE TOO YOU ENCOUNTER AN EXPERIENCE RELATIVELY UNCHANGED IN DECADES, CENTURIES EVEN.

Of the city's once numerous secondhand markets a dozen or so survive, still busy and full of life despite rent hikes and periodic clampdowns on fly pitches. The flea markets, in common with some of the shops covered in the first three chapters of this book, sell run-of-the-mill used stuff – mobile phone chargers, Hoovers, furniture and frying pans. Brick Lane, Deptford and Nine Elms all fall into this category. Other markets are newer, catering to the vintage crowd, sometimes specifically with clothes but often with furniture, lighting and homeware too. A third variety, long established in Bermondsey, Portobello Road, Covent Garden and Camden Passage, are labelled as 'Antiques' markets, but also sell much in the way of secondhand 20th century goods, and are duly included here.

At the flea markets the action starts early, and regular punters know to arrive before the crowds to get the best bargains. The undignified hours are usually soothed by the presence of some fantastic food stalls set up alongside the secondhand stalls. Vintage markets, and most of the antiques markets, keep more respectable hours.

£££-£££

COVENT GARDEN ANTIQUES MARKET

Jubilee Hall, off Southampton Street, Covent Garden WC2 8BD
Mon 5:00-16:00
Covent Garden Tube

Few of the stalls at the Monday Antiques market in Covent Garden sell antiques as such. They're more in the collectibles and ephemera mould, featuring everything from old magazines and newspapers through to ceramics and military medals. Housed in the large undercover space of the Jubilee Hall, it's a busy, varied market, its authenticity perhaps unexpected in the heart of a London tourist hotspot.

The market has a preponderance of jewellery stalls, from cheap costume jewellery to more expensive pieces in silver and gold. A few bric-a-brac traders sell everything from paintings and mirrors

to dressmakers' dummies and Dr Martens boots. The dealers in magazines and newspapers always have a good audience, sifting through old copies of *Picturegoer* or examining a 1942 edition of the *Evening News*; 'Position improves at Stalingrad' reads the headline. Elsewhere, old postcards, cutlery, clocks, spectacles, food tins, watches and clocks comprise just some of the ephemera on sale. A clutch of fast-food joints, hovering over the market on a first floor balcony, are hard to ignore when lunchtime approaches.

There's an addendum to the Monday Antiques Market just to the north of Jubilee Hall, in the Apple Market part of Covent Garden, where more secondhand jewellery traders rub shoulders with a stall selling old cameras, another dealing in letterpress blocks and various stalls selling silverware. Old phones, from the early 20th century candlestick style to the coloured 700 series of the 1960s, all in working order, occupy another stall.

GRAYS ANTIQUE MARKET

**58 Davies Street and 1-7 Davies Mews,
Mayfair W1K 5AB
0207 629 7034
www.graysantiques.com
Mon-Fri 10:00-18:00; Sat 11:00-17:00
Bond Street Tube**

As the name implies, the focus at Bennie Gray's historic central London operation is chiefly on antiques, with fine jewellery and watches taking centre stage. However, there's more than a sniff of interest for the dedicated secondhand and vintage shopper in the shape of costume jewellery, vintage clothing, old toys and dolls, prints, magazines and other collectibles. The remnants of the river Tyburn flowing through the basement of the main building brings a mild thrill to any visit. See chapters one, two and three for more info on specific traders.

PORTOBELLO ROAD MARKET

£££-£££

Portobello Road, Notting Hill
Antiques Market: Sat
Under Westway (clothes): Fri-Sun
Golborne Road (furniture/homeware):
Mon-Sat
Notting Hill Gate/Ladbroke Grove/
Westbourne Park Tubes

Like Camden and Brick Lane, Portobello Road Market comprises various different sections. In common, the secondhand elements set up on a Saturday, when the long road swarms with people heading north in a slow tide that starts at Notting Hill Gate.

The **Antiques Market** is the first stretch encountered, running down the hill in front of the multiple antique shops and arcades that made Portobello Road iconic. Most traders are, as you'd expect, antique dealers, but there are more prosaic goods on sale here too, from vintage toys to bits of furniture, crockery and cameras. The antique arcades off to the side of the market, the Portwine Galleries in particular, are well worth a visit if you're after collectibles (toys, radios and musical instruments sit alongside more traditional 'antiques').

The best section of the market for secondhand clothes, bric-a-brac and the like begins half a mile further up Portobello Road, past the fruit and veg stalls and the buskers to where the Westway rumbles overhead. A dozen or so stalls reside under the Westway itself, one selling everything from old table lamps to alarm clocks, keyboards and more. Another has antique and costume jewellery; and a third, old gramophones. The Gramophone Stall has been a Portobello fixture since 1975. "Young people seem fascinated by them," says proprietor, Jill, stood behind three portable pre-war turntables. "They can't believe you don't need batteries; that you just wind them up and the sound comes out." The stall also sells 78s, needles and old postcards.

Walk left under the Westway's flank, **down to Ladbroke Grove**, and you're eventually rewarded with half a dozen secondhand clothes stalls. The quality here is very good, with tweeds, wax jackets, fur and Burberry Macs in abundance, and prices that undercut many of the area's equivalent shops. Back toward Portobello Road, a canopied area between the Westway and Cambridge Gardens harbours what is perhaps London's most concentrated patch of secondhand clothes traders. Some stalls have their areas of expertise, from 1980s Adidas tracksuits and fur coats to military paraphernalia (need a genuine fire hood?), although most simply sell pre-millennium men's and women's clothes at goodish prices.

The patches of Portobello where the market turns flea-like all happen off to the right-hand side as you head north. The first is just past the Westway, where a friendly mix of stalls and fly pitches sell secondhand shoes, bikes, tins, toys, record players and more. Further up Portobello Road, on the right-hand corner with Raddington Road, a stretch of rather forlorn pavement-side stalls sell old junk, from vacuum cleaners to suitcases. Finally, the best and biggest flea market attached to Portobello is on **Golborne Road** (turn right with the Trellick Tower in your sights), historically a separate market where bric-a-brac sellers lay out their furniture and random collections of stuff in crates on the roadside. This is where the bargains are to be had. The local, longstanding Portuguese and Moroccan communities ensure that browsing is accompanied by the wonderful smells of frying fish.

🕒 £ £

BACKYARD MARKET

The Old Truman Brewery, next to
146 Brick Lane, Shoreditch E1 6QL
0207 770 6020
www.backyardmarket.co.uk
Sat 11:00-18:00; Sun 10:00-18:00
Liverpool Street Tube/
Shoreditch High Street Overground

Part of the Old Truman Brewery complex, the young(ish) Backyard Market occupies a spacious, light warehouse set slightly back from Brick Lane. It's a 50/50 split between secondhand clothes stalls and indie designers, although a great used camera seller sets up amid the food stalls near the entrance. The clothes are cheap but less refined than in Brick Lane's vintage boutiques. Keep an eye out for the guy who makes things (clocks, coasters, ashtrays) from old 45 records.

BRICK LANE MARKET

Shoreditch
Sun 9:00-mid afternoon
Shoreditch High Street Rail/
Aldgate East Tube

Brick Lane sprawls out a colourful market every Sunday morning to the north of its railway bridge. Tennis racket, drill, lamp, book, lawnmower – you'll find a secondhand variant of almost anything on Brick Lane and the roads that lead off it. The stallholders, in keeping with the area's rich history, are drawn from myriad cultures.

Rather than one continuous flea market, Brick Lane is a sporadic affair, the stalls clustered in four or five distinct clumps. Recent developments, not least to the neighbouring railway line, have changed the market's shape, and no doubt will do so again in the near future. Indeed, the market evolves by the week. For all the changes, it remains a vibrant and pleasingly anarchic place.

On **Brick Lane** itself the market stalls are at their most ordered. The mix of goods is broad. One trader sells secondhand bikes, many with a nearly new gleam. Another sells gas masks and Barbie dolls (the connection seems unclear). However, most of the secondhand stalls (woven amid fruit and veg stalls and traders selling new goods) are bric-a-brac, a mix of furniture, music and clothes, all dusted off and peddled as 'vintage'. The market peters out at the railway bridge. South of this, passing players busy on Carrom Boards and the old Truman Brewery, the road heads into Banglatown.

On the streets leading off Brick Lane the pockets and stretches of market are more ramshackle; the goods and the prices less buffed. **Sclater Street** begins with a few stalls on the right hand side. Some are fly pitches, as basic as a blanket laid on the pavement and lined with pairs of old football boots; others are fully fledged record and clothes stalls. One trader sells old coffee bean sacks. Further down Sclater Street, the small, cramped patches of waste ground on either side comprise the scruffy heart of Brick Lane's secondhand market. You can find anything here: bikes, clothes, books, comics, toys, games consoles, computers, phone chargers, cassette tapes – all sold with no questions asked under makeshift blue tarp roofs.

The Brick Lane end of **Cheshire Street** is lined with vintage clothes boutiques, and the stalls that gather in front on a Sunday morning mirror their content with racks of pre-loved clobber. The clothes aren't as choice as the ones you'll find in the shops, but the prices are lower. Further down Cheshire Street, half a dozen secondhand hardware stalls take up residence in the small cul-de-sac of Hare Marsh. Garden rakes, pans and lawnmowers are sold from the back of a truck, whilst another seller lays out vacuum cleaners and household ephemera on a blanket. Opposite, a trader offers up bike wheels. If you're in the market for a secondhand leaf blower, this is the place to come.

Finally, as Cheshire Street heads down towards the Valance Road, there's an **indoor market** on the right hand side, where the Brick Lane experience is at its most flea-like. One trader sells a mind-boggling array of power tools; another displays secondhand watches; a third has a mix of vacuum cleaners, televisions and jewellery.

BRICK LANE

Brick Lane and the surrounding area has a compelling history. In Roman times it was a burial ground, placed just outside the city walls. Its current name emerged in the 16th century, derived from the lane's brick factory. As a notoriously poor area of London, the road soon became – and long remained – a magnet for migrants newly arrived in London. First came the Huguenots, master weavers fleeing persecution on the Continent in the early 1700s. Then the Irish, in the late 18th century. Jewish migrants arrived in the late 1880s, before, in the second half of the 20th century, the lane changed guise again, christened Banglatown with its new residents arrived from the Subcontinent.

Brick Lane has also had its darker moments. Number 13 used to be the Frying Pan, the pub where Mary Ann Nichols was last seen before Jack the Ripper got to her. A later victim, Annie Chapman, was found in Hanbury Street, just off Brick Lane. On Cheshire Street, leading off the northern end of the Lane, the Kray twins bought the Carpenter's Arms pub for Violet, their mum. Reggie apparently stopped in for Dutch courage on his way to murdering Jack 'The Hat' McVitie in 1967. The pub's still there.

OLD SPITALFIELDS MARKET

16 Horner Square, Spitalfields EC1 6EW
0207 247 8556
www.oldspitalfieldsmarket.com
Mon-Fri 10:00-16:00; Sun 9:00-17:00
Liverpool Street Tube

Spitalfields is perhaps the most polished of London's old markets, its covered, historic home rejuvenated nearly a decade ago to accommodate market stalls alongside stylish clothing boutiques, shops and restaurants. Some bemoan the sanitisation, rising rents and loss of stall space, but most will confirm that the spruced up Spitalfields remains a vibrant, interesting place.

There's usually a bric-a-brac or vinyl stall to be found in amongst the arts, crafts and clothes that predominate in the market irrespective of what day you go there. However, Thursday and Sunday are the prime days for secondhand shopping. On Thursday the Antique Market unfurls, its traders seemingly drawn from across southern England, peddling furniture, homeware, old toys, books, clothes and jewellery. Don't be put off by the name, much of the merchandise is 'retro/vintage' rather than antique. On Sunday the secondhand clothes and jewellery stalls come out, boosted by the solid crowds that visit this part of London for the attendant market and shops in Brick Lane. The secondhand traders sit well alongside the fashion students selling their latest designs. See chapter two for details of the bi-monthly record fair held in Old Spitalfields Market.

SUNDAY UPMARKET

Ely's Yard, The Old Truman Brewery,
Brick Lane, Shoreditch E1 6QL
0207 770 6028
www.sundayupmarket.co.uk
Sun 10:00-17:00
Liverpool Street Tube/
Shoreditch High Street Overground

The Old Truman Brewery cooked up its last pint two decades ago. Today it's an evocative, hip complex of shops, studios, bars and eateries, at its most vibrant on a Sunday when the large indoor Upmarket unravels. Secondhand clothes (well priced and varied), magazines and vinyl stalls are thick on the ground, lining up amid exotic food stalls, Banksy prints and designers selling new clothes and jewellery.

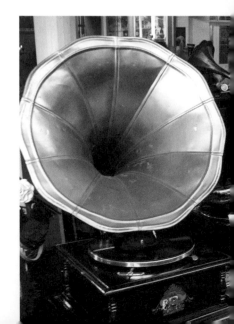

ALFIES ANTIQUE MARKET

13-25 Church Street, Marylebone NW8 8DT
0207 723 6066
www.alfiesantiques.com
Tue-Sat 10:00-18:00
Marylebone/Edgware Road Tube

Bennie Gray bought the old Jordan's department store in Marylebone's Church Street in 1976. The site was derelict but the stylish façade and fixtures of the building remained. After revamping the building, he opened Alfies, a centre for antiques traders, which, four decades on, is amongst the best places in London to find early to mid 20th century furniture, lighting, clothes, posters and prints. There are genuine antiques here too (most of them in the jewellery, watch and ceramic shops of the ground floor), but fewer than in Bennie's other indoor market (Grays), off Bond Street.

You can lose two or three hours meandering the old levels and stairways of the atmospheric late 19th century building, exploring the 70 or so dealers dispersed across four floors. Whilst the collectibles, books and jewellery are laudable, it's the breadth of interior design that really sets Alfies apart (see earlier chapters in the book for further details of particular traders.) A rooftop café rewards anyone working their way up through the building, and there's even a hair salon, Nina's Hair Parlour, dedicated to vintage dos.

ⓔ£₤-ⓔ£₤
THE CAMDEN MARKETS

Camden High Street
Mon-Sun approx 10:30-18:00
Camden Town/Chalk Farm Tube

The markets in Camden (there are five main sites, working north from Camden Town Tube: Inverness Street, Buck Street Market, Camden Lock Village Market, Camden Lock and the Stables) have developed apace since the 1970s. They're not quite the counterculture dens of old, with landlords, redevelopments and tourism all having an impact.

Many of the old secondhand and vintage traders have graduated from stalls to more permanent units in the covered markets. Indeed, the majority of Camden's secondhand stuff is now sold from established shops within the vast Stables Market complex, Camden Lock Market and in the shops along Camden High Street. Some of the best of these are covered elsewhere in this book.

The stalls that set up along **Inverness Street**, the suffocating warren of **Buck Street Market** (fronting onto Camden High Street with a giant green 'Camden Market' sign), or just over the river in the **Village Market**, all sites once home to vintage clothing stalls, no longer seem to sell secondhand goods. In **Camden Lock**, the original Camden market, established as a craft market in 1974, the stalls in the Central Hall, Middle Yard and West Yard harbour a couple of well-priced used vinyl stalls, but little more for the secondhand shopper. The vintage stuff, from clothes and accessories to books, resides in the Lock's permanent shops.

Only in the dark heart of the old **Stables Market**, in the newly renovated Horse Tunnels, will you find anything resembling a flea market. The atrium of the Tunnels is packed tight with stalls. One sells chandeliers, a handful have homeware and other bits of crockery, and another, King's Prints, sells old maps, lithographs and magazine adverts. The Baggage Room is one of two stalls piled high with old leather cases, 'steamer' trunks and other slices of high 20th century society – wooden tennis rackets, Box Brownies and the like. The Horse Tunnels are also home to a tiny but superb stall crammed with Dinky Routemasters, Star Wars figures and other old toys.

Camden Markets run all week, the exception being the **Electric Ballroom** next to the Tube station, its film and record fairs (on certain Saturdays) and secondhand clothes stalls (Sundays) pitching up on the sticky floor of its nightclub host on weekends only. Most of the Camden markets are quiet during weekdays, idling along before the chaotic but enjoyable scrum that unfurls every Sunday.

CAMDEN PASSAGE MARKET

Off Upper Street, Islington N1 8EF
Wed and Sat 8:00-16:00
www.camdenpassageislington.co.uk
Angel Tube

The unpretentious antiques and curios stalls of Camden Passage, a genteel Islington side street, have been camping out here twice a week since the 1960s. They're fewer in number than of old (rent hikes and the recent demise of the nearby Mall Antiques Arcade have dented the area's reputation as an antiques hub), but varied nonetheless. Gilded mirrors and chandeliers share pavement space with soupspoons, tea sets, gurning statuettes and rugs. A number of other stalls sell vintage clothes and jewellery, but miscellaneous *objets* remain the Camden Passage life force.

Three covered areas lend the market a sense of permanence; the southernmost serving as a gateway to Pierrepoint Arcade, a loop of claustrophobic but colourful secondhand shops stocked with ceramics, lights, antiques and ephemera. The shops along Camden Passage itself are more polished, selling quality vintage clothes and mid-range antiques. The street also has a good choice of cafés and watering holes

GRAFTON SCHOOL MARKET

Approach via Hercules Place, off Seven Sisters Road, Holloway N7 6AR
Sat 8:00-16:00; Sun 10:00-14:30
Holloway Road Tube

A stone's throw from Nag's Head Market but a separate affair, the large weekend markets in the playground of this Holloway Primary School attract a loyal crowd, queuing at the gates to get in. On Saturday it's roughly a 50/50 split between old and new goods; on Sunday, the emphasis is on secondhand. The market recalls a bygone London in which, by necessity, nothing was wasted. Microwaves, beat-up trainers, video players, three-piece suites, mobile phone chargers, frocks – it's all here, and it's all sold for next to nothing. As one regular punter comments, exaggerating only mildly, "it saves it going to landfill."

NAG'S HEAD MARKET

22 Seven Sisters Road, Holloway N7 6AG
Wed 8:00-17:00; Sun 6:00-early pm
Holloway Road Tube

Some of the dozen or so stalls camped in the old yard behind the Nags Head general market on Seven Sisters Road are there all week, but the best days for secondhand activity are Wednesday and Sunday. On the latter it's a genuine flea market, the stalls selling a mix of clothes, crockery, books, DVDs, silverware, jewellery and chintzy ornaments. The goods here are cheap and, by and large, deserve to be. However, a handful of the stalls are of genuine interest. One includes three crates of vinyl, another has a dozen or so collectible cameras sold by a guy who knows his stuff, and a third specialises in old postcards, stamps and medals.

NINE ELMS MARKET

New Covent Garden Market, Nine Elms Lane,
Nine Elms SW8 5BH
Sun 8:00-15:00
Vauxhall Tube/Battersea Park Rail

Pick your way from Nine Elms Lane through the car parks and concrete blocks that surround New Covent Garden Market on a Sunday and you'll find Nine Elms Market. It's big and ugly, but also exciting and chock-full of life. About 80 percent of the stalls sell new goods; the remaining portion, mostly arranged at either end of the long central section of the market, proffers anything and everything secondhand. There aren't many markets where you can leave clutching a chainsaw, a frying pan and a cuddly toy. But Nine Elms is that market. It has what must be London's largest collection of secondhand electrical stalls, selling everything from laptops to drills, freezers to guitar amps, car stereos and televisions. A couple of stalls sell old bikes and their constituent parts; one or two more sell rather unremarkable secondhand clothes. The most interesting stalls for bric-a-brac are to be found undercover in the garages at the easternmost end of the site. If you're willing to rummage there are bargains to be had in here, on furniture, pictures, books and other random oddments.

NORTHCOTE ROAD ANTIQUES MARKET

155A Northcote Road, Battersea SW11 6QB
0207 228 6850
Mon-Sat 10:00-18:00; Sun 12:00-17:00
Clapham South Tube/ Wandsworth Common
Rail/Clapham Junction Rail

Packed snugly into one two-storey building, roughly midway between the commons of Clapham and Wandsworth, Northcote Road is an unpretentious permanent market comprising 25 or so traders. A lot of the silverware and jewellery and some of the furniture is genuine antique, but equally, there's much here from the first half of the 20th century, from old flour tins and soda fountains through to chandeliers and pine tables. It's a good place for decorative glass and objet d'art rather than surprises or bona fide bargains.

🄔🄕🄕-🄔🄕🄕

BERMONDSEY ANTIQUES MARKET

Bermondsey Square, Southwark SE1
www.bermondseysquare.co.uk/antiques
Fri 5:00-13:00
London Bridge/Borough Tube

Some may lament the great shrinking of Bermondsey Antiques Market, but others will celebrate the more manageable scale of what is a Friday morning institution. This part of south London is mid spruce-up, a process that has cleared out much of the market, as well as the antique arcades and shops that used to gather around its fringe, but which has also arguably improved the quality of what's on sale. Where once there were hundreds of stalls, today about two dozen remain, selling a boiled down mix of antiques (there's a lot of silverware and jewellery--both costume and antique) and objects of interest, none of it junk.

One stall has a fine collection of mid 20th century mantel clocks, jewellery boxes, cutlery and candlesticks. Another has a box of old cameras, some of them pre-war, and an earthenware jug labelled 'Domestos'. A number of traders hawk kitchenware and glass; others sell paintings or bits of ivory, shaped into shoehorns, bookmarks and the like. Given the changes wrought in recent years, the market has done well to retain such a friendly atmosphere, even while its popularity with tourists has probably led to above average prices.

HYMIE BLECHMAN

"Come on then Sir, I'll give you a pound if you can tell me what's inside this stick." Hymie Blechman offers an impish smile, slowly unscrewing the egg-shaped head of a walking stick, drawn from a pot of ten or so on sale in front of a table topped with old postcards, silver candle sticks and bits of carved ivory. "Now think. It's something you're not supposed to do; something naughty." Out comes a thin white tube. Hymie screws the tube into the egg-shaped top and, job done, puts the assembled pipe into his mouth. His pound remains firmly in pocket.

Hymie has been setting up his stall at Bermondsey Market for 46 years, here every Friday at four in the morning. He drives up from his antiques shop in Bournemouth. "There used to be 300 stalls here," he says. "Now there are about 30. But it's still a good market, and to be honest, making it smaller has cleared out some of the junk – the stuff that couldn't be sold." He's typical of the traders at Bermondsey. Most have been coming here for decades, arriving insanely early to cater for 'trade' customers, some of whom no doubt take their catch back to Portobello Road or Camden Passage.

🌐£££

DEPTFORD
FLEA MARKET

Douglas Way, Deptford SE8 4AG
Sat morning
New Cross Tube/ Deptford Rail

Deptford's flea market leads off the brilliant, multicoloured general market that pulsates down Deptford High Street on a Saturday. It runs along Douglas Way, behind the Albany, a performing arts centre. It's an honest-to-goodness affair, an antidote, should you need one, to the knowing professionalism of London's more famous flea markets.

Large tables are piled high with all goods known to man, from coat hangers to builder's hats, mirrors to tins of paint. Ask the traders for a price. Some of the more organised stalls are vaguely themed: used laptops, keyboards and other IT debris; chandeliers and jewellery; furniture; gardening equipment; and washing machines. But many comprise arbitrary piles of things, be they golf clubs, hamster cages, hats, tennis rackets, bottles of suntan lotion, toasters or sewing machines. The far end of the market is marked by an old railway luggage trolley piled high with shoes and surrounded by visitors trying to find a matching pair, for which they'll pay £1. Sift through the junk – and there are mountains of it – and you'll undoubtedly find something of use, possibly even value.

GREENWICH CLOCKTOWER MARKET

166 Greenwich High Road, Greenwich
SE10 8NN
www.clocktowermarket.co.uk
Sat-Sun 10:00-17:00
Greenwich DLR/Cutty Sark DLR

Laid back and friendly, the Clocktower Market sets up on a small patch of tarmac just up the road from the main Greenwich Market, past the Picturehouse on the left. It's a mix of jewellery, homeware, vintage sunglasses, clothes, books, bags and paintings and prints; the downsized survivor of larger, more flea-like markets that used to reside in Greenwich.

Jewellery takes up the lion's share here, much of it cheap. Everything on the secondhand book stall sells for £1, whether it's the *Fab Annual 1981* or *Anne of Windy Willows*. Paul, resplendent in kilt and white woollen waistcoat, sells fine men's vintage clothes, including suits that date back to the 1920s. He offers an adjustment service. "If you're buying an old suit, it won't fit perfectly," he explains. "You might need to adjust the length, put the shoulders right and so on. But what you will get, almost without exception, is a better quality suit than anything new you can buy."

Lyn's stall has piles of old buttons. Art deco, Edwardian, modern, brass, abalone, bakelite – there are thousands, all drawn from Lyn's own collection. "We recycle, we Womble it up," she smiles, nodding at her husband Ray, who runs the adjoining vintage tool stall. "Tools are a very personal thing," offers Ray, behind an array of wooden handled chisels, brass spirit levels and saws. Can't argue with that.

Where Camden and Portobello can be overwhelming at times, the Clocktower Market at Greenwich is pleasingly manageable. The crowds are reduced and the prices a shade lower too. Back in the bustling heart of Greenwich, the main covered Market has its vintage, antiques and collectibles days on a Thursday and Friday, 10am to 5.30pm.

LONDON CAR BOOT SALES

In case you haven't been initiated into the wonderful world of the car boot sale, it runs thus: members of the public pile anything they want to sell (from snowboarding boots to unidentified Rembrandts) into the back of their car; they then drive to an organised event (in London that usually means a car park or a school playground), pay the car boot guv'nor for a pitch, open said boot, possibly erecting a trestle table in front, and commence selling. The car boot sales of London comprise a number of well-established weekly or monthly events:

BATTERSEA CAR BOOT SALE

Battersea Park School, Battersea Park Road, Battersea SW11 5AW
Sun 13:30-17:30
www.batterseaboot.com
Battersea Park Rail

CAPITAL CAR BOOT

Pimlico Academy, Lupus Street, Pimlico SW1V 3AT
Sun 12:30-16:00
www.capitalcarboot.com
Pimlico Tube

CHELSEA WALK-IN BOOT SALE

Chelsea Theatre, World's End Place,
King's Road, Chelsea SW10 0DR
Last Sunday of the month, 13:00-16:00
www.chelseatheatre.org.uk
Fulham Broadway Tube

CHISWICK CAR BOOT SALE

Chiswick Community School, Burlington
Lane, Chiswick W4 3UN
First Sunday of the month, 8:00-13:00
(except Jan)
Chiswick Rail

ST AUGUSTINE'S CAR BOOT SALE

St Augustine's School, Kilburn Park Road,
Kilburn NW6 5SN
Sat 11:00-15:00
www.thelondoncarbootco.com
Kilburn Park Tube

ST MARY'S CAR BOOT SALE

St Mary's Primary School, Quex Road,
Kilburn NW6 4PG
Sat 10:00-15:00
www.thelondoncarbootco.com
Kilburn Park Tube

SOUTHFIELD PRIMARY CAR BOOT SALE

Southfield Primary School, Bedford Park,
Chiswick W4 1BD
Last Sunday of the month (Feb to Nov),
8:30-12.30
Turnham Green Tube

STOKE NEWINGTON CAR BOOT

Princess May School, Princess May Road,
Stoke Newington N16 8DF
Sat 9:00-15:00; Sun 9:00-14:00
www.thelondoncarbootco.com
Dalston Kingsland Rail

WIMBLEDON CAR BOOT SALE

Wimbledon Greyhound Stadium, Plough
Lane, Wimbledon SW17 0BL
Wed 10:30-14:00; Sat 6:30-13:30;
Sun 7:00-13:30
Wimbledon Park Tube

LONDON CHARITY SHOPS

Charity shops have long played a role on London's streets. Odorous jokes aside, they've always been places to sniff out a bargain, where bohemians and hard-up pensioners rummage side by side. However, the growth of London's vintage and retro shops over the last decade has crowded the charity shops' territory somewhat. And yet, in straitened times, there are still thousands around London, and a handful still have a reputation for hidden treasure. As might be expected, the quality objects or designer clothes are more likely to surface in affluent areas. It's also worth noting that some charity shops, like Oxfam's chain of Boutiques, have evolved into something new with the rise of vintage fashion. Here are five charity shops to whet the appetite:

BRITISH RED CROSS

69-71 Old Church Street, Chelsea SW3 5BS
South Kensington Tube

One of two British Red Cross shops in London selling designer clothes and accessories from the likes of Vivienne Westwood and Nicole Farhi (the other one is in Victoria).

FARA KIDS

662 Fulham Road, Fulham SW6 5RX
0207 013 0744
Parsons Green Tube

A charity shop wholly devoted to the sale of children's clothes, toy, books and nursery equipment. FARA also runs a shop for grown-ups on Fulham Road, at number 841.

GERANIUM SHOP FOR THE BLIND

8A Earls Court Road, Kensington W8 6EA
0207 795 6166
High Street Kensington Tube

Rifle through the stuff that Kensington discards and you might turn up a designer dress or a retro leather jacket. Also good for a few books and bits of bric-a-brac.

OXFAM BOUTIQUE

190 Chiswick High Road, Chiswick W4 1PP
0208 994 4888
Turnham Green Tube

One of a handful of Oxfam Boutiques in London selling carefully selected vintage pieces alongside designs made from secondhand clothing and fabric by a team of young designers.

TRAID

661 Westbourne Grove, Notting Hill W2 4UA
0207 221 2421
Bayswater/Royal Oak Tube

Something of a legend amongst charity shops, Traid in Westbourne Grove has a reputation for vintage and designer clothes. Proceeds help fight exploitation in the global textile supply chain.

LONDON AUCTIONS

Bonhams, Christie's and Sotheby's are the best known of inner London's auction houses, renowned for the sale of fine art and antiques, but there are others, no less exciting, that sell more prosaic secondhand goods, from old sofas to ballroom chandeliers.

CHISWICK AUCTIONS

1 Colville Road, Chiswick W3 8BL
0208 992 4442
www.chiswickauctions.co.uk
Every Tue at 12:00
South Acton Rail

An antiques and fine art auctioneer that also deals in contemporary items and designer goods, selling everything from collectible toy trains to sketches by John Constable. A favourite with the antique hunting shows on TV.

CRITERION AUCTIONS

41-47 Chatfield Road, Wandsworth SW11 3SE,
and 53 Essex Road, Islington N1 2SF
0207 228 5563/0207 359 5707
www.criterionauctioneers.com
Every Mon at 17:00 (at both sites)
Clapham Junction Rail/Angel Tube

Criterion have weekly auctions in both Islington and Wandsworth, selling off a nicely rounded mix of antiques and more contemporary items, including furniture, jewellery and art.

FRANCIS SMITH LTD

107 Lots Road, Chelsea SW10 0RN
0800 195 7800
www.francissmith.co.uk
Every Tue at 18:15
Fulham Broadway

Historic auction house selling antiques, many of them Victorian, but with some 20th century pieces of special merit included alongside.

FRANK G BOWEN

253 Joseph Ray Road, Leytonstone E11 4RA
0208 556 7930
www.frankgbowen.co.uk
Every other Thu at 11:00
Leytonstone Tube

You can find all sorts at Bowens, from bikes to watches to clothes and iPods, most of it sourced from the police, insolvency practitioners, lost property companies and bailiffs. Say no more.

GENERAL AUCTIONS

Garratt Mills, Trewint Street, Wandsworth SW18 4HA
0208 870 3909
www.auction.u-net.com
Usually held on the 1st and 3rd
Monday of the month at 11:00
Earlsfield Rail

A lot of vehicles go under the hammer at the Garratt Mills site, but punters can also bid on nearly new computers, televisions, jewellery and other 'general' stuff.

GREASBY'S

211 Longley Road, Tooting SW17 9LG
0208 672 2972
www.greasbys.co.uk
Every other Tue at 10:00
Tooting Broadway Tube

Greasby's sell off bikes, engineering equipment, luggage, mobile phones, hair dye and other miscellaneous stuff for the likes of HM Revenue & Customs and airline operators.

GREENWICH AUCTIONS

47 Old Woolwich Road, Greenwich SE10 9PP
0208 853 2121
www.greenwichauctions.co.uk
Every Sat at 11:00
Cutty Sark DLR

A bit of everything goes under the hammer at the large Greenwich Auction rooms, from chesterfields to thermos flasks and old copies of *The Dandy*. The premises include a permanent furniture, lighting and collectibles sale centre, open seven days a week.

LONDON
MAPS

The following collection of maps will help you navigate your way around London's secondhand and vintage shops and markets. Each corresponds to the zones used in the preceding chapters – West, East, North, Southwest and Southeast. Where the spacing of the shops and markets demands it, the maps have been subdivided into more detailed areas (alas, London's streets rarely conform to neat patterns!).

Each entry is listed under its category and the colour of the icon on the map corresponds to that category, with sites marked by diamonds:

CLOTHES AND ACCESSORIES

BOOKS, MUSIC & MEMORABILIA

HOME & GARDEN

ONLY IN LONDON

A select handful of cafés are marked by a:

Each map has a QR code. If you have a smart phone, you can simply scan the code to link to online versions of the maps on Google which will help you find your way around. These are regularly updated to keep pace with London's evolving secondhand and vintage landscape.

CLOTHES ◆
BOOKS & MUSIC ◆
HOME & GARDEN ◆
ONLY IN LONDON ◆

Somers Town

Regent's Park

Euston Road

Euston Square

Warren Street

Great Portland Street

Regent's Park

Park Crescent

Portland Place

Great Portland Street

Great Portland Street

Regent St

Marylebone

Fitzrovia

Mortimer Street

Gower Street

Tottenham Court Road

Goodge Street

Bloomsbury

Russell Square

Russell Square Gardens

Woburn Place

Bernard Street

Guilford

Southampton Row

13 18

Oxford Street

Oxford Circus

Oxford Street

Bond Street

9 3 4
5

Regent Street

4

6

Soho

Shaftesbury Avenue

Chinatown

Tottenham Court Road

St Giles

15 14
20 11 12

New Oxford Street Bloomsbury Way

High Holborn

Holborn

2

10

7

Covent Garden

Long Acre

Kingsway

Strand Und

Mayfair

Leicester Square

19
16

Piccadilly Circus

Piccadilly

Regent Street

Haymarket

Charing Cross

Strand

Strand 7 Strand

Embankment

Golden Jubilee Bridge

Cockspur Street

St James's Street

Pall Mall

Pall Mall

1000ft

Green Park

200m

Piccadilly

The Mall

Whitehall

Embankment

Green Park

CLOTHES

1 AUSTIN KAYE
425 Strand WC2R 0QE.
Mon-Fri 9:30-17:30;
Sat 9:30-17:00

2 BLACKOUT II
51 Endell Street, Covent Garden
WC2H 9AJ. Mon-Fri 11:00-19:00;
Sat 11:30-18:30; Sun 12:00-17:00

3 DIANE HARBY
148 Grays Antiques Market,
Davies Street, W1K 5LP.
Mon-Fri 10:00-18:00

4 FUR COAT NO KNICKERS
Top Floor, Kingly Court, Carnaby
Street W1B 5PW. Mon-Sat 11:00-
19:00 (Tue 11:00-17:30);
Sun 12:30-17:00

5 GILLIAN HORSRUP
Inside Vintage Modes, Grays
Antiques Market, 1-7 Davies Mews,
W1K 5AB. Mon-Sat 11:00-17:00

6 MARSHMALLOW MOUNTAIN
Ground Floor, Kingly court
(off Carnaby St), London W1B 5PW.
Mon-Wed 11:00-19:00; Thu-Sat
11:00-20:00, Sun 12:00-18:00

7 ROKIT
42 Shelton Street, Covent Garden,
WC2H 9HZ. Mon-Sat 10:00-19:00;
Sun 11:00-18:00

8 ROWAN AND ROWAN
315 Grays Antique Market,
58 Davies St, W1K 5LP.
Mon, Wed and Fri 10:00-17:00

9 VINTAGE MODES
Grays Antiques Market,
1-7 Davies Mews, W1K 5AB.
Mon-Fri 10:00-18:00

10 THE VINTAGE SHOWROOM
14 Earlham Street, WC2H 9LN.
Mon-Sat 11:30-19:30;
Sun 12:00-17:00

BOOKS & MUSIC

11 APERTURE CAMERA CAFE
44 Museum Street, WC1A 1LY.
Mon-Fri 11:00-19:00; Sat 12:00-19:00

12 CAMERA CITY
16 Little Russell Street, WC1A 2HL.
Mon-Fri 10:00-17:30;
Sat 10:30-14:00

13 CEX
32 Rathbone Place, Fitzrovia W1T
1JJ. Mon-Wed, Sat, 10:00-19:30;
Thu-Fri 10:00-20:00;
Sun 11:00-19:00

14 THE CLASSIC CAMERA
2 Pied Bull yard (off Bury Place),
WC1A 2JR. Mon-Fri 9:45-17:30;
Sat 10:00-16:30

15 COINCRAFT
44 & 45 Great Russell Street,
WC1B 3LU. Mon-Fri 9:30-17:00;
Sat 10:00-14:30

16 COLIN NARBUTH AND SONS
20 Cecil Court, off Charing Cross
Road, WC2N 4HE. Tue-Fri 10:30-
17:30; Mon-Sat 10:30-16:00

17 GAY'S THE WORD
66 Marchmont Street, Bloomsbury,
WC1N 1AB. Mon-Sat 10:00-18:30;
Sun 14:00-16:00

18 HOBGOBLIN MUSIC
24 Rathbone Place, W1T 1JA.
Mon-Sat 10:00-18:00

19 MARCHPANE
16 Cecil Court, off Charing
Cross Road WC2N 4HE.
Mon-Sat 11:00-18:00

20 OXFAM BLOOMSBURY
12 Bloomsbury Street, WC1B 3QA.
Mon-Sat 10:00-18:00;
Sun 12:00-17:00

21 A PLACE IN SPACE
237 Shaftesbury Avenue WC2H
8EH. Mon-Wed 10:30-18:30; Thu-Sat
10:00-19:00; Sun 10:00-16:00

22 RG GRAHAME
129/130 Grays Antique Market,
28 Davies Street, W1K 5LP.
Mon-Fri 11:00-17:00

23 R:G. LEWIS
29 Southampton Row, London,
WC1B 5HL. Mon-Fri 8:30-17:00;
Sat 9:30-17:45

24 SAX
21 Denmark Street WC2H 8NA.
Mon-Fri 10:00-18:00;
Sat 10:00-17:00

25 SISTER RAY RECORDS
34-35 Berwick Street, Soho,
W1F 8RP. Mon-Sat 10:00-20:00;
Sun 12:00-18:00

26 SKOOB
66, The Brunswick, off Marchmont
Street, WC1N 1AE. Mon-Sat 10:30-
20:00; Sunday 10:30-18:00

27 SOUNDS OF THE UNIVERSE
7 Broadwick Street, Soho,
W1F 0DA. Mon-Sat 11:00-19:30

28 TRAVIS AND EMERY
17 Cecil Court, off Charing Cross
Road WC2N 4EZ.
Mon-Sat 10:15-18:45;
Sun 11:30-16:30

29 VINTAGE AND RARE GUITARS
6 Denmark Street WC2H 8LX.
Mon-Sat 10:00-18:00;
Sun 12:00-16:00

30 VINTAGE MAGAZINE SHOP
39-43 Brewer Street, Soho,
W1F 9UD. Mon-Wed 10:00-19:00;
Thu 10:00-20:00; Fri-Sat 10:00-
22:00; Sun 12:00-20:00

HOME & GARDEN

31 POP BOUTIQUE
6 Monmouth Street,
Covent Garden WC2H 9HB.
Mon-Sat 11:00-19:00;
Sun 13:00-18:00

ONLY LONDON

32 GRAYS ANTIQUE MARKET
58 Davies Street and 1-7 Davies
Mews, W1K 5AB. Mon-Fri 10:00-
6:00; Sat 11:00-17:00

33 COVENT GARDEN ANTIQUES MARKET
Jubilee Hall, off Southampton
Street, Covent Garden, WC2 8BD.
Mon 5:00-16:00

CAFÉ

34 BAR CHOCOLATE
27 D'Arblay Street, Soho W1V 3PF

WEST
WEST LONGON

CLOTHES ◆
BOOKS & MUSIC ◆
HOME & GARDEN ◆
ONLY IN LONDON ◆

CLOTHES

1 **282**
282 Portobello Road, W10 5TE.
Tue-Sun 12:00-17:00

2 **295**
295 Portobello Road, W10 5TD.
Fri-Sat 8:30-17:00

3 **DOLLY DIAMOND**
51 Pembridge Road, Notting Hill
Gate, W11 3HG. Mon-Fri 10:30-
18:30; Sat 9:30-18:30;
Sun 12:00-18:00

4 **HORNETS**
36B Kensington Church Street
W8 4BX. Mon-Sat 11:00-18:00

5 **JANE BOURVIS**
89 Golborne Road,
North Kensington, W10 5NL.
Tue-Sat 10:30-18:00

6 **RELLIK**
8 Golborne Road,
North Kensington W10 5NW.
Tue-Sat 10:00-18:00

7 **ONE OF A KIND**
259 Portobello Road, W11 1LR.
Mon-Sun 10:00-18:00 (18:30 on Sat)

8 **ORSINI**
76 Earls Court Road, Kensington
W8 6FQ. Mon-Sat 10:30-18:00;
Sun 12:00-17:00

9 **RETRO WOMAN (DESIGNER SHOP)**
20 Pembridge Road,
Notting Hill Gate, W11 3HL.
Mon-Sun 10:00-20:00

BOOKS & MUSIC

10 **ADRIAN HARRINGTON RARE BOOKS**
64a Kensington Church Street,
Kensington W8 4DB.
Mon-Sat 11:00-17:00

11 **BOOK AND COMIC EXCHANGE**
14 Pembridge Road,
Notting Hill Gate, W11 3HT.
Mon-Sun 10:00-20:00

12 **CLASSICAL MUSIC EXCHANGE**
36 Notting Hill Gate, W11 3HX.
Mon-Sun 10:00-20:00

13 **INTOXICA**
231 Portobello Road, W11 1LT.
Mon-Sat 10:30-18:30;
Sun 12:00-17:00

14 **STAGE AND SCREEN**
34 Notting Hill Gate, W11 3HX.
Mon-Sun 10:00-20:00

15 **CLASSICAL MUSIC EXCHANGE**
36 Notting Hill Gate, W11 3HX.
Mon-Sun 10:00-20:00

CONTINUED

HOME & GARDEN

16 **LAST PLACE ON EARTH**
305-307 Portobello Road, W10 5TD.
Mon-Sun 11:00-17:00

17 **THE OLD CINEMA**
160 Chiswick High Road, W4 1PR.
Mon-Sat 10:00-18:00;
Sun 12:00-17:00

18 **OLLIE & BOW**
69 Golborne Road, North
Kensington, W10 5NP.
Tue-Sat 10:00-17:00 (Closed Thu)

19 **X ELECTRICAL**
125 King Street, Hammersmith
W6 9JG. Mon-Sat 10:00-18:00

ONLY LONDON

20 **CHISWICK AUCTIONS**
1 Colville Road, Chiswick W3 8BL.
Every Tuesday at 12:00

21 **CHISWICK CAR BOOT SALE**
Chiswick Community School,
Burlington Lane W4 3UN.
First Sunday of the month,
8:00-13:00 (except Jan)

22 **GERANIUM SHOP FOR THE BLIND**
8A Earls Court Road,
Kensington W8 6EA

23 **GOLBORNE ROAD MARKET**
Golborne Road, Kensington.
Mon-Sat

24 **OXFAM BOUTIQUE**
190 Chiswick High Road,
Chiswick W4 1PP

25 **PORTOBELLO ANTIQUES MARKET**
Portobello Road. Saturday

26 **PORTOBELLO FLEA MARKET**
Under the Westway, Portobello
Road. Fri-Sun

27 **SOUTHFIELD PRIMARY
CAR BOOT SALE**
Southfield Primary School,
Bedford Park, Chiswick W4 1BD.
Last Sunday of the month
(Feb to Nov), 8:30-12:30

28 **TRAID**
661 Westbourne Grove,
Notting Hill W2 4UA

EAST
SHOREDITCH / BRICK LANE

CLOTHES ◆
BOOKS & MUSIC ◆
HOME & GARDEN ◆
ONLY IN LONDON ◆

Shoreditch

Hoxton

Dunloe Street

Crondall Street

Pitfield Street

Regan Way

Hoxton Street

Geffrye Court

Stanway Street

Dunloe Street

ckney Road

ipton Stre

Columb

Elw

W

Kingsland Road

Waterson Street

Pelter Street

Columbia Road

Chambord Street

Drysdale Street

Austin Street

Calvert Avenue

Arnold Circus

Swanfield Street

Brick Lane

Chilton Street

Boot Street

Old Street

Charlotte Road

Rivington Street

Shoreditch High Street

Bateman's Row

New Inn Yard

Old Nichol Street

Club Row

Chance Street

Redchurch Street

Redchurch Street

Bacon Street

Willow Street

Blackall Street

Rave Street

Great Eastern Street

Leonard Street

Luke Street

Pitfield Street

Scrution Street

Clifton Street

Holywell Row

Curtain Road

Bethnal Green Road

Sclater Street

Shoreditch High Street

Quaker Street

Buxton Street

Calvin Street

Grey Eagle Street

Commercial Street

Brick Lane

Spital Street

Pindar Street

Appold Street

Primrose Street

Folgate Street

Hanbury Street

anbury Street

Princelet Street

Hanbu

Spelman Street

rl Street

eet

Brushfield Street

Heneage Street

500ft
100m

CLOTHES

1 ABSOLUTE VINTAGE
15 Hanbury Street, E1 6QR.
Mon-Sun 11:00-19:00

2 DIRTY BLONDE
66A Cheshire Street, E2 6EH.
Thu-Sat 11:00-18:00;
Sun 11:00-18:00

3 HUNKY DORY
226 Brick Lane, Shoreditch E1 6SA.
Mon-Sun 11:30-18:30

4 LEVISONS
1 Cheshire Street, E2 6ED.
Mon-Sun 12:00 until late

5 PAPER DRESS
114-116 Curtain Road, Shoreditch,
EC2A 3AH. Mon-Sat 10:30-19:30;
Sun 12:00-18:00

6 SKEWIFF AND SCATTY
64 Sclater Street, E1 6HR.
Thu-Sun; mid morning until late

7 THE VINTAGE EMPORIUM
14 Bacon Street, Shoreditch E1 6LF.
Mon-Sun 10:00-19:00
(café 10:00-20:00)

BOOKS & MUSIC

8 DUKE OF UKE
22 Hanbury Street, Shoreditch,
E1 6QR. Tue-Fri 12:00-19:00;
Sat-Sun 11:00-18:00

9 SPITALFIELDS RECORD FAIR
Old Spitalfields Market, Spitalfields,
E1 6EW. First and third Friday of
the month 10:30-16:30

HOME & GARDEN

10 BACON STREET SALVAGE
12 Bacon Street, Shoreditch E1 6LF.
Mon-Sun 9:00-17:00

11 C.E. BURNS & SONS
16-22 Bacon Street, Shoreditch
E1 6LF. Mon-Fri 9:00-16:00;
Sat 9:00-13:00

12 ELEMENTAL
67 Brushfield Street, Spitalfields,
E1 6AA. Tue-Sun 11:00-18:00

13 LE GRENIER
146 Bethnal Green Road, Shoreditch
E2 6DG. Mon-Sat 12:00-19:00
(closed Wed); Sun 10:00-19:00

14 SECONDHAND LOCK-UP
Railways Arches, Brick Lane,
Shoreditch. Mon to Sun 8:00-18:00

15 THE SECOND HAND STORE
14 Bacon Street, Shoreditch, E1 6LF.
Mon-Sun 11:00-17:00

16 THE TEA ROOMS
The Old Truman Brewery,
next to 146 Brick Lane, E1 6QL.
Sat 11:00-18:00; Sun 10:00-17:00

17 VINTAGE HEAVEN
82 Columbia Road, Bethnal Green
E2 7QB. Fri by appointment;
Sat 12:00-18:00; Sun 8:30-17:00

18 WESTLAND
St Michael's Church, Leonard
Street, EC2A 4ER. Mon-Fri
9:00-18:00; Sat 10:00-17:00

ONLY LONDON

19 BACKYARD MARKET
The Old Truman Brewery,
next to 146 Brick Lane, E1 6QL.
Sat 11:00-18:00; Sun 10:00-18:00

20 BRICK LANE MARKET
Shoreditch. Sunday 9:00-mid
afternoon

21 OLD SPITALFIELDS MARKET
16 Horner Square, Spitalfields
EC1 6EW. Mon-Fri 10:00-16:00;
Sun 9:00-17:00

22 SUNDAY UPMARKET
Ely's Yard, The Old Truman
Brewery, Brick Lane, E1 6QL.
Sun 10:00-17:00

CAFÉ

23 BRICK LANE COFFEE
157 Brick Lane, Shoreditch E1 6SB

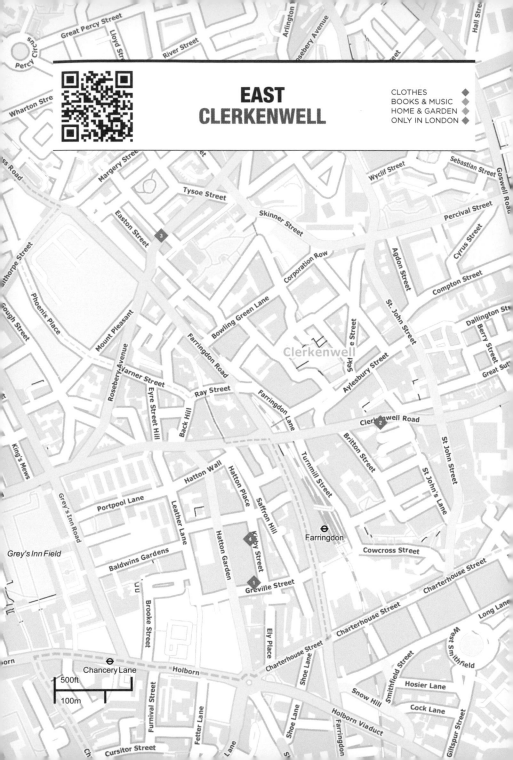

EAST CLERKENWELL

CLOTHES ◆
BOOKS & MUSIC ◆
HOME & GARDEN ◆
ONLY IN LONDON ◆

CLOTHES

1 ANDREW R ULLMANN LTD
36 Greville Street, London,
EC1N 8TB. Mon-Sat 10:00-17:00

2 ANTIQUE WATCH CO
19 Clerkenwell Road EC1M 5RS.
Mon-Fri 11:00-16:30

**3 CLERKENWELL VINTAGE
FASHION FAIR**
The Old Finsbury Town Hall,
Rosebury Avenue, EC1R 4RP. Eight
fairs a year (always on a Sunday)

4 HIRSCHFELDS
Suite 26, 88-90 Hatton Garden
EC1N 8TE. Mon-Fri 8:00-17:00

NORTH CAMDEN

CLOTHES ◆
BOOKS & MUSIC ◆
HOME & GARDEN ◆
ONLY IN LONDON ◆

CLOTHES

1 A DANDY IN ASPIC
Unit D13 Horse Tunnel Market
and Unit 566 Stables Market, both
Chalk Farm Road, Camden NW1
8AH. Mon-Fri 11:00-18:30;
Sat-Sun 10:00-19:00

2 CRISTOBAL
26 Church Street, Marylebone NW8
8EP. Tue-Sat 10:30-16:30

3 CAMDEN THRIFT STORE
51 Chalk Farm Road, Camden NW1
8AN. Mon-Sun 12:30-18:30

4 CAMDEN VINTAGE
Unit D10/11 Horse Tunnel Market,
Chalk Farm Road, Camden.
NW1 8AH. Mon-Sun 11:00-18:00

5 GENERAL EYEWEAR
Arch 67, Stables Market, Chalk
Farm Road, Camden NW1 8AH.
Tue-Thu 12:00-18:00;
Sat-Sun 10:00-18:00

BOOKS & MUSIC

6 BLACK GULL BOOKS
70 West Yard, Camden Lock,
NW1 8AF. Mon-Sun 10:00-18:00

7 DODO
First Floor, Alfies Antique Market,
13-25 Church Street,
Marylebone NW8 8DT.
Tue-Sat 10:30-17:30

8 PSYCHOTRONIC
30D Second Floor Market Hall,
Camden Lock NW1 8AL. Wed, Thu,
Sat, Sun 13:00-18:00

9 RESURRECTION RECORD
228 Camden High Street,
Camden, NW1 8QS.
Mon-Sun 10:30-17:45

10 WALDEN BOOKS
38 Harmood Street, Camden NW1
8DP. Thu-Sun 10:30-18:30

HOME & GARDEN

11 ATOMIUM
Unit D18, Horse Tunnel Market,
Chalk Farm Road, Camden NW1
8AH. Thu 12:00-17:00;
Fri-Sun 10:30-18:00

12 BETH
Ground Floor, Alfies Antique
Market, 13-25 Church Street,
Marylebone NW8 8DT.
Tue-Sat 10:00-17:00

13 CAMDEN CYCLES
251 Eversholt Street, Camden, NW1
1BA. Mon-Fri 9:00-19:00; Sat 9:00-
18:00; Sun 11:00-17:00

14 CURIOSITY
Unit 90C, Stables Market,
Camden NW1 8AH.
Mon to Fri 11:00-19:00;
Sat to Sun 10:00-19:00

15 DECORATUM
In the basement of Alfies Antique
Market, 13-25 Church Street,
Marylebone NW8 8DT.
Tue-Sat 10:00-18:00

16 PRIMROSE HILL INTERIORS
115 Regents Park Road, Primrose
Hill NW1 8UR.
Tue-Sat 11:00-18:00;
Sun 12:00-17:00

17 STEPHEN LAZARUS
First Floor, Alfies Antique Market,
13-25 Church Street,
Marylebone NW8 8DT.
Mon-Sat 10:00-17:00

18 VINCENZO CAFFARELLA
Ground Floor, Alfies Antique
Market, 13-25 Church Street,
Marylebone NW8 8DT.
Tue-Sat 10:00-18:00

19 VINTAGE PLANET
Unit D23 Horse Tunnel Market,
Chalk Farm Road,
Camden NW1 8AH.
Mon-Fri 12:00-18:30;
Sat-Sun 10:30-19:00

ONLY LONDON

20 ALFIES ANTIQUE MARKET
13-25 Church Street,
Marylebone NW8 8DT.
Tue-Sat 10:00-18:00

21 CAMDEN LOCK MARKET
Camden High Street.
Mon-Sun Approx 10:30-18:00

22 CAMDEN STABLES MARKET
Camden High Street. Mon-Sun
Approx 10:30-18:00

23 ELECTRIC BALLROOM
Camden High Street.
Sat and Sun

24 ST AUGUSTINE'S CAR BOOT SALE
St Augustine's School, Kilburn Park
Road NW6 5SN. Sat 11:00-15:00

25 ST MARY'S CAR BOOT SALE
St Mary's Primary School,
Quex Road, Kilburn NW6 4PG.
Sat 10:00-15:00

CAFÉ

26 MY VILLAGE CAFÉ
37 Chalk Farm Road,
Camden NW1 8AJ

CLOTHES ◆
BOOKS & MUSIC ◆
HOME & GARDEN ◆
ONLY IN LONDON ◆

Crouch Hill

Stroud Green

Upper Tollington Park

Manor House

Finsbury Park

Blackstock Road

Brownswood Road

Green Lanes

Clissoid Park

Stoke Newington

Stoke Nast

No

Seven Sisters Road

Parkland Walk

Tollington Road

Arsenal

Highbury Park

Albion Road

Kingsland Road

Lower Holloway

Holloway Road

Highbury Grove

Highbury Fields

Green Road

Dalston Kingsla

Holloway Road

Liverpool Road

Paradise Park

Saint Paul's Road

New Islington Green Road

Balls Pond Road

Dalston Junc

Dalston

Highbury and Islington

Highbury

Canonbury Road

Caledonian Road and Barnsbury

Barnsbury

Southgate Road

De Beauvoir Town

Essex Road

Bernard Park

New North Road

Regent's Canal towpath

Kingsland Road

Islington

Haggerston

2000ft

500m

Hoxton

Shepherdess

Hoxton

CLOTHES

1 21ST CENTURY RETRO
162 Holloway Road, N7 8DD.
Mon-Sat 10:00-18:00;
Sun 11:00-18:00

2 ANNIE'S
12 Camden Passage, Islington
N1 8ED. Mon-Sun 11:00-18:00

BOOKS & MUSIC

3 AQUAMARINE
14 Pierrepont Row, Camden
Passage, Islington N1 8EF.
Wed and Sat 9:00-17:30; Mon, Tue,
Thu-Fri and Sun 12:00-17:30

4 CHURCH STREET BOOKSHOP
142 Stoke Newington Church
Street, N16 0JU.
Mon-Sun 11:00-18:00

5 ELDICA
8 Bradbury Street, Dalston
N16 8JN. Tue-Sat 11:30-19:00;
Sun 12:00-19:00

6 FLASHBACK
50 Essex Road, Islington N1 8LR.
Mon-Sat 10:00-19:00;
Sun 12:00-18:00

7 HAGGLE VINYL
114 Essex Road, Islington, N1 8LX.
Mon-Sun 10:00-18:00

8 LUCKY SEVEN (AND LUCKY PAD)
127 Stoke Newington Church
Street, N16 0UH.
Mon-Sun 11:00-19:00

9 VINCENT FREEMAN
1 Camden Passage, Islington
N1 8EA. Wed/Sat 10:30-16:30;
or by appointment

HOME & GARDEN

10 THE ARCHITECTURAL FORUM/N1 ARCHITECTURAL SALVAGE
312-314 Essex Road, Islington
N1 3AX. Mon-Sat 10:00-17:15

11 AUDIO GOLD
308-310 Park Road, Crouch End
N8 8LA. Mon-Sat 10:30-18:30

12 THE COBBLED YARD
1 Bouverie Road, Stoke Newington,
N16 0AH. Tue-Sun 11:00-18:00

13 MR ALL SORTS
191 Northchurch Road, Islington
N1 3NT. Mon-Sat 9:00-18:00

14 ODYSSEY
1 Pierrepoint Arcade, Camden
Passage, Islington N1 8EF. Wed
9:00-15:30; Thu/Fri 13:00-18:00;
Sat 9:00-17:00; Sun 13:00-18:00

15 OOH-LA-LA!
147 Holloway Road, N7 8LX. Mon
11:00-18:00; Tue-Sat 10:00-18:00

16 PELICANS AND PARROTS
40 Stoke Newington Road, Dalston,
N16 7XJ. Mon-Fri 12:00-20:00;
Sat 11:00-20:00; Sun 12:00-19:00

17 SARGENT AND CO
74 Mountgrove Road,
Finsbury Park N5 2LT.
Wed-Sat 10:30-18:30

18 THE SECOND HAND YARD
Marton Road (the Church Street
end), Stoke Newington, N16 0RA.
Wed-Sun early until late

ONLY LONDON

19 CRITERION AUCTIONS (ISLINGTON)
53 Essex Road, Islington N1 2SF.
Every Monday at 17:00

20 CAMDEN PASSAGE MARKET
Off Upper Street, Islington N1 8EF.
Wed and Sat 8:00-16:00

21 GRAFTON SCHOOL MARKET
Approach via Hercules Place,
off Seven Sisters Road, Holloway
N7 6AR. Sat 8:00-16:00;
Sun 10:00-14:30pm

22 NAG'S HEAD MARKET
22 Seven Sisters Road, Holloway
N7 6AG. Wed 8:00-17:00;
Sun 6:00-early pm

23 STOKE NEWINGTON CAR BOOT
Princess May School, Princess May
Road, Stoke Newington N16 8DF.
Sat 9:00-15:00; Sun 9:00-14:00

CAFÉ

24 THE BLUE LEGUME
101 Stoke Newington Church Road,
Stoke Newington N16 0UD

25 THE ELK IN THE WOODS
39 Camden Passage,
Islington N1 8EA

SOUTHWEST

CLOTHES ◆
BOOKS & MUSIC ◆
HOME & GARDEN ◆
ONLY IN LONDON ◆

Paddington
Oxford Street St Giles
Soho
Chinatown
Bayswater Road
Bayswater Road
Mayfair

Victoria
South Kensington
South Kensington
Glouchester Road
Earls Court
Victoria
2
West Kensington
Sloane Square
Barons Court
Pimlico
Pimlico
10
West Brompton
9
Vauxhall
Chelsea Embankment
Vauxhall
6
Fulham Broadway
11
Chelsea Embankment
Oval
Fulham
14
17
Kennington
13
Parsons Green
Imperial Wharf
Battersea
Stockwell
New King's Ro.
8
Putney Bridge
7
Stockwell
1
12
Stockwell
Putney Bridge
Clapham Junction
Lavender Hill
Clapham North
East Putney
Clapham Junction
Clapham
Brixton
5
West Hill
Wandsworth
St. Johns Hill
Clapham Common
Brixton 3
Acre Lane
Brixton
18
Southfields
Clapham South
Southfields
Balham
Brockwe
15
Wimbledon Park
Balham
Wimbledon Park
4
Tooting Bec
Streatham Hill
19
Tooting Bec Common
2000ft
1km
Tooting
Streatham
16
Tooting Broadway
Wimbledon
Colliers Woods
Streatham Common

CLOTHES

1 OLD HAT VINTAGE
66 Fulham High Street, SW6 3LQ.
Mon-Sat 10:30-18:30

2 RETROMANIA
6 Upper Tachbrook Street, Pimlico,
SW1V 1SH. Mon-Sat 10:00-18:00;
Sun 11:00-17:00

BOOKS & MUSIC

3 BOOKMONGERS
439 Coldharbour Lane,
Brixton SW9 8LN.
Mon-Sat 10:30-18:30

4 MY BACK PAGES
8-10 Balham Station Road,
Balham SW12 9SG. Mon-Sat
10:00-19:00; Sun 11:00-18:00

HOME & GARDEN

5 COLLECTIBLES
82 Brixton Village, off Coldharbour
Lane, Brixton SW9 8PS.
Wed 11:00-15:00; Thu 10:00-22:00;
Fri 10:00-18:00; Sat 10:00-20:00;
Sun 11:00-16:30

6 LASSCO
Brunswick House, 30 Wandsworth
Road, Vauxhall SW8 2LG. Mon-Sat
10:00-17:00; Sun 11:00-17:00

7 NEW VINTAGE
256 Battersea Park Road, Battersea
SW11 3BP. Mon-Wed 11:30-18:00;
Thu 11:30-18:30; Fri 12:00-18:00;
Sat 10:30-18:00; Sun 12:00-17:00

ONLY LONDON

8 BATTERSEA CAR BOOT
Battersea Park School, Battersea
Park Road SW11 5AW.
Sun 13:30–17:30

9 BRITISH RED CROSS
69-71 Old Church Street,
Chelsea SW3 5BS

10 CAPITAL CAR BOOT
Pimlico Academy, Lupus Street
SW1V 3AT. Sun 12:30-16:00

11 CHELSEA WALK-IN BOOT SALE
Chelsea Theatre, World's End
Place, King's Road SW10 0DR. Last
Sunday of the month, 13:00-16:00

**12 CRITERION AUCTIONS
(WANDSWORTH)**
41-47 Chatfield Road, Wandsworth
SW11 3SE. Every Monday at 17:00

13 FARA KIDS
662 Fulham Road, Fulham
SW6 5RX

14 FRANCIS SMITH LTD
107 Lots Road, Chelsea SW10 0RN.
Every Tuesday at 18:15

15 GENERAL AUCTIONS
Garatt Mills, Trewint Street,
Wandsworth SW18 4HA.
Usually held on the 1st and 3rd
Monday of the month at 11:00

16 GREASBY'S
211 Longley Road, Tooting SW17
9LG. Every other Tue 10:00

17 NINE ELMS MARKET
New Covent Garden Market,
Nine Elms Lane SW8 5BH.
Sun 8:00-15:00

**18 NORTHCOTE ROAD ANTIQUES
MARKET**
155A Northcote Road, Battersea
SW11 6QB. Mon-Sat 10:00-18:00;
Sun 12:00-17:00

19 WIMBLEDON CAR BOOT SALE
Wimbledon Greyhound Stadium,
Plough Lane SW17 0BL. Wed 10:30-
14:00; Sat 6:30-1:30; Sun 7:00-13:30

SOUTHEAST
WATERLOO

CLOTHES ◆
BOOKS & MUSIC ◆
HOME & GARDEN ◆
ONLY IN LONDON ◆

Holborn

London Wall

Holborn Viaduct

Chance

Farringdon

Soundsditch

wych

and

Victoria Embankment
Temple

Blackfriars Underpass
Paul's Walk

Upper Cannon Street
Lower Thames Street

Monument

Tower

Blackfriars Bridge

Bankside

London Bridge

Bridge bridge

South Bank

Southwark Bridge Road

Stamford Street

Southwark Street

London Bridge

Tooley Street

Stamford Street

Southwark Street

Borough

Tooley St

York Road

Waterloo

The Cut

Union Street

Southwalk

Southwark

Blackfr

Waterloo Road

Borough

Long Lane

Bermondsey Street

Druid Street

Tower Bridge Road

3   7

Baylis Road

Borough Street

2

4

Borough Road

Harper Road

Great Dover Street

Abbey Street   Ab

Lambeth North

London Road

Harper Road

St George's Road

Elephant & Castle

New Kent Road

Grange Road

Lambeth Road

Kennington Road

Elephant and Castle

Newington Butts

Walworth Road

Old Kent Road

Kennington Lane

Walworth

Kennington Park Road

Kennington

Walworth Road

6

1000ft

200m

Kennington
Oval

Kennington Park

Camber

Albany Road

Burgess Park

CLOTHES

1 RADIO DAYS
87 Lower Marsh, Waterloo SE1 7AB.
Mon-Sat 10:00-18:00

2 WHAT THE BUTLER WORE
131 Lower Marsh, Waterloo
SE1 7AE. Mon-Sat 11:00-18:00

BOOKS & MUSIC

3 GRAMEX
25 Lower Marsh, Waterloo SE1 7RJ.
Mon-Sat 11:00-19:00

4 SECONDHAND BOOKS
20 Lower Marsh, Waterloo SE1 7RJ.
Wed-Fri 11:00-19:00

5 SOUTHBANK BOOK MARKET
Under the arches of Waterloo
Bridge. Mon-Sun late
morning-early evening

HOME & GARDEN

6 BLUE MANTLE
The Old Fire Station,
306-312 Old Kent Road SE1 5UE.
Mon-Sat 10:30-17:30;
Sun 2:30-18:30pm (or by appt)

ONLY LONDON

7 BERMONDSEY ANTIQUES MARKET
Bermondsey Square,
Southwark SE1.
Fri 5:00-13:00

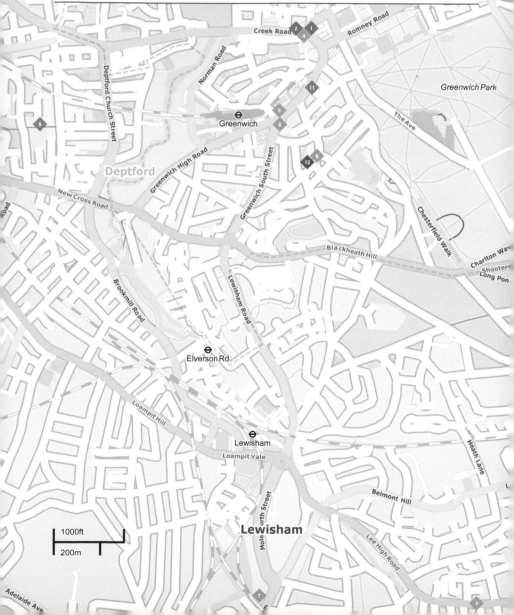

SOUTHEAST GREENWICH

CLOTHES ◆
BOOKS & MUSIC ◆
HOME & GARDEN ◆
ONLY IN LONDON ◆

CLOTHES

1 **EMPORIUM**
330-332 Creek Road,
Greenwich, SE10 9SW.
Wed-Sun 10:30-18:00

2 **UMI AND CO VINTAGE**
320-322 Creek Road, Greenwich
SE10 9SW. Tue-Fri 10:30-18:00;
Sat 10:30-18:30;
Sun 12:00-18:00

BOOKS & MUSIC

3 **ALLODI ACCORDIONS**
143-145 Lee High Road, Lewisham
SE13 5PF. Mon 14:00pm-18:00;
Tue, Thu and Fri 10:30-18:00;
Sat 10:30-17:00

4 **CASBAH RECORDS**
(At the Beehive), 330-332 Creek
Road, Greenwich SE10 9SW.
Mon-Sun 10:30-18:00

5 **HALCYON BOOKS**
1 Greenwich South Street,
Greenwich SE10 8NW.
Mon-Sat 10:00-18:00

6 **NAVAL AND MARITIME BOOKS**
66 Royal Hill, Greenwich SE10 8RT.
Wed-Sat 10:00-18:00

7 **ROBERT MORLEY PIANOS**
34 Engate Street, Lewisham
SE13 7HA. Mon-Sat 9:30-17:00

HOME & GARDEN

8 **THE JUNK SHOP AND SPREAD EAGLE**
9 Greenwich South Street,
Greenwich, SE10 8NW.
Mon-Sun 10:00-18:00

ONLY LONDON

9 **DEPTFORD FLEA MARKET**
Douglas Way, Deptford SE8 4AG.
Sat morning

10 **GREENWICH AUCTIONS**
47 Old Woolwich Road, Greenwich
SE10 9PP. Every Sat at 11:00

11 **GREENWICH CLOCKTOWER MARKET**
166 Greenwich High Road,
Greenwich SE10 8NN.
Sat-Sun 10:00-17:00

CAFÉ

12 **BUENOS AIRES CAFÉ AND DELICATESSEN**
86 Royal Hill, Greenwich SE10 8RT

LONDON
INDEX OF SHOPS